Seductions, Lies and Good Intentions

Seductions, Lies and Good Intentions

Memoirs of My Life Online

Layne Underwood

iUniverse, Inc.
New York Lincoln Shanghai

Seductions, Lies and Good Intentions
Memoirs of My Life Online

iUniverse books may be ordered through booksellers or by contacting:

iUniverse
2021 Pine Lake Road, Suite 100
Lincoln, NE 68512
www.iuniverse.com
1-800-Authors (1-800-288-4677)

ISBN-13: 978-0-595-37778-7 (pbk)
ISBN-13: 978-0-595-82153-2 (ebk)
ISBN-10: 0-595-37778-5 (pbk)
ISBN-10: 0-595-82153-7 (ebk)

Printed in the United States of America

Contents

Hi! That's me, the screwed up little kid sitting in an inch of cold bath water. What's even sadder is that I had to crop my little brother out of the photo. He was sitting on the other side with his back to me. In my family it was apparently okay to bathe together as long as you weren't looking at each other. It wasn't until thirty years later that I found a possible reason for the lack of water in our bathtub and the reason why we were tucked into bed at night with our arms above the covers.

After her death, I found among my grandmother's things a book first published in 1917 by William J. Robinson, M.D. it was republished in 1936 by Eugenics Publishing Company, New York. The title
—Woman: Her Sex and Love Life.

My grandmother was a teacher and my mother a nurse yet I grew up with no understanding of sexuality. After reading Dr. Robinson's book I have to assume the teacher and the nurse took the author/doctor's word as God's gospel. My limited knowledge was gained through skewed bible teachings and my voyeuristic hours spent in the barnyard. At the beginning of my chapters I will be sharing pieces of Dr. Robinson's book. I enjoy what usually contradicts today's thinking and also the parts that still hold true. Enjoy!

*   *   *   *   *

The child-boy or girl-should sleep alone, on a rather hard mattress. The covering should be light. A coverlet may be put over the feet. The child always should sleep with the arms out upon the cover or blanket, never under the same. If this is done from childhood on, it is very easy to get used to this way of sleeping, and many a case of masturbation will thus be obviated. The child should not be permitted to loll in bed: it must be taught to get up as soon as it awakes in the morning. The general bringing-up must be of a strengthening, hardening character; and this applies both to the body and the will. When the children reach the age of nine, ten, eleven, twelve or thirteen years (we must use discrimination and judgment, for, some children of nice are as developed as are others of thirteen), we must tell them that it is bad and injurious to handle one's genitals, and we must warn them to shun any companions who wish to initiate them into any manipulations of these parts or who show an inclination to talk about the sexual organs and sex matters.

Hot baths are very injurious for young children in their influence in this direction. There is no question that a hot bath has a very decided stimulating affect upon the sexual desire of adults as well as on children, both male and female; in fact, I have had several patients of either sex tell me that their first masturbatory act was committed while they were in a hot bath.

Woman: Her Sex and Love Life

My Journey

It's said that a journey of a thousand miles begins with a single step. Mine began with a simple "click," taking me farther than I had ever even imagined I wanted to go.

It was the summer of my divorce, and I emerged from the dark days of oppressive monogamy (at least on my part) with eyes half closed, my vision obscured. Odd how long it can take to adjust when first exposed. Tempting…tempting to crawl back into the familiar dark of my past, but I had decided to force myself to live.

I suppose choosing to live would sound like such an obvious thing to someone whom has never experienced depression, someone who grew with the knowledge that they had a lot to offer the world. I grew up being a dreamer, but I was a closet dreamer. I said little, kept to myself and dared not disrespect my elders by telling them I was Somebody. When I got such lofty notions, I was made fun of and laughed at…so I'd retreat back into my shell. I'd try to be who they thought I should be. I tried. I was miserable.

With adolescence came rebellion. I was the black sheep, and I reveled in it. When I was out doing things that I knew would make my parents crazy, it felt like the weight that held me down had been lifted. The proverbial millstone no longer attached, I soared. My visions of being someone well known and respected allowed me to express myself. I stood taller and straighter…I had friends. I trusted my friends.

Confidence allowed me to date. I felt loved, cared for, cherished. I met another. He was funny; cocky…he hung out with the wrong crowd. My parents hated him, so I had to have him. He said he loved me. I got pregnant. I was sixteen. I truly believe that it wasn't a purposeful act, not even subconsciously…but it happened, and it was the kind of thing that a respected religious family couldn't deny. The bad girl had done a bad thing, and the whole world could see it. I decided to have the baby and prove I hadn't made a mistake. After graduating from high school I would marry the bad boy and we would be a happy family. I was sure I could make that happen.

I do. I did. I promised to love, honor and obey, till death do us part, in the presence of God and about 400 witnesses. There, it was set; my whole life promised to the loving and honoring of one man. I was a wife and a mother. It was my life; cooking, cleaning, caring for our daughter, and college…what more could

1

an eighteen year old want? I've blocked most of the memories from those first few years of marriage. We would fight every day. The dreamer in me…comatose. A good husband would have sat by the dreamer's bedside, held her hand and begged her to come back. Mine wanted to unplug the life support machines.

The facade went on for nearly fourteen years. My stubborn side determined to be the woman my husband wanted. Home was hell when he was around. In front of my friends and family, all was fine. I put on my happy face and made excuses if they questioned anything. Behind closed doors, I cried, screamed, begged for him to love me. 'Til death do you part…hmm…now there's an option; I could end my suffering. But, my daughter…I couldn't leave her. I lived for her. Maybe I'd get lucky and he'd die. He liked to ride dirt bikes. When he first started the new hobby, I worried so that he would get hurt. Now I encouraged him to jump higher, drive faster…and went so far as to suggest that the helmet obscured his vision.

He lived. I struggled to still be the one he wanted. He cheated. He threw it in my face and it nearly destroyed me. Cheating was the one thing I wouldn't put up with and I didn't. My eyes were opened on a Saturday…by that Tuesday, he had divorce papers served on him. I was free, but I felt dead.

Who was I? At that time, I don't believe I knew. Being stubborn, I thought I knew, or I tried to give the outward appearance of knowing. Yet, I was a wreck. I was an empty shell. I was a divorcee. I was the waste product of a bad decision gone wedlock. Holy matrimony, what's a girl to do?

The beginning…yes, beginning. Funny; at the time, it felt like my end. How a strong-willed individual lets herself be controlled baffles me…or at least it did. I was her. I was that sheepish being who feared confrontation so much I just lowered my head and nodded agreement when my husband suggested anything. I let myself believe that I was not good enough, smart enough, thin enough or talented enough to live outside of what was then my existence. Now I shall celebrate not the end of her, but the beginning of ME!

I was about to discover myself. The dreamers eyes fluttered…the coma was about to end! It was terrifying to be a "newborn" at thirty-two…terrifying, but exciting.

Thinking back on my childhood and marriage (they kind of ran together since I married at eighteen), I led a very simple, careful, quiet, caterpillar life. If someone brushed up against me, I curled into a ball, hoping to go unnoticed. The months of tears, anger and hibernation after my husband left, were my chrysalis. Of course when you are in the cocoon, it looks more like a tomb than a necessary part in your development, but without it I would have never found my wings. Wings I learned to spread, wings that longed for the light, wings that gave me freedom to soar. Wings that allowed me…my butterfly years.

The fundamental part of human nature-the desire for happiness and the avoidance of suffering-cannot be changed, nor would we want to change it if we could. It would mean the disappearance of the human race. But that many of our primitive emotions can be greatly modified by culture, by new standards, by new ideals of morality, about this there can be no question.

Woman: Her Sex and Love Life

Lonely Lady

How do I pull myself together after building my life around someone who now tells me smugly, "I only said that I loved you because that's what you wanted to hear. I've purposely been mean and horrible to you for the last four years because I wanted you to kick me out." Excuse me? He wanted me to kick him out? Yes, I had wanted him to tell me that he loved me...every day I wanted to hear it—I needed to hear it—but the whole point was to be reassured that he did love me, not to just hear the words. When *I* said it, *I* meant it. Yes. I'm sure I had meant it; after all, I would have never left.

Tears...buckets and buckets of tears, box after box of tissues, rivers of self-pity; puffy eyes, blotchy skin, nasty hair, and a PMS 24/7 kind of attitude. Baggy clothes, an old recliner, blankets and the remote (HA! At least now I can hold the remote!) What an ugly road I am turning down. I endure days and days of nothingness. Why live...what is there to live for?

I don't eat. I can't eat. Placing food in my mouth only brings back memories of Dickhead looking at me and saying "You really need to eat that?" or "Haven't you had enough?" When I try to eat something, my throat won't let me swallow it. The food begins to taste rancid and I need to go and throw it up. I just try to sleep away as many painful minutes of my life as possible. I begin to think death would be a relief, a way to put an end to the heartbreak and embarrassment. I can't even go to the grocery store. Going would show the world that I was now alone...people would know...they could see...I'm sure they could tell. It's a small town and I have no doubts that all 4,000 inhabitants are already aware of the fact that I am such a loser that I can't even keep my husband. No, I won't subject myself to their snickering behind my back; I don't need any food. I am too fat to deserve to eat anyway...I will just continue not eating.

Why is life so cruel? Why do I always have to be the one in pain? I should just give up…yes, death would be easy…that would teach him…wouldn't it? If they found me dead and knew it was because of the pain he had caused me…he would be sorry. Then he would know he was wrong to leave me. Everyone would know that he was wrong.

My dark, lonely little world has a bright spot—my daughter, my most miraculous achievement, a gleaming ray of hope in my dense universe. Amazingly, she loves me. She really cares about me and she comforts me…she can even get me to smile a little. Oh, a smile…what an incredible thing! This house used to be full of smiles…at least that's how I remember it to have been. Now I don't want to smile, I want to be miserable. I *am* miserable. I am alone. Yet there she is, my reason for living, my greatest hope. I must really pull myself together; I have to pull it together, after all…SHE might still need me. I have to remember what she would have left without me…him and his new love…aaaccckkkk…I can't leave my dearest possession with them!

Amber is in the next room. The room behind my recliner, the filthy, cluttered office with the computer in it. She spends hours "online" talking with friends. Friends that she has never met, who are teens like her, teens with the same likes, dislikes and problems she has. Boys who tell her they like her, or maybe even love her. They send her e-cards; computer generated flower bouquets, jokes, virtual kisses, audio files and all kinds of things that brighten her days. How can a bunch of silly, cold computer-generated words and pictures seem to excite her so much? I don't understand. I tell her she is nuts…doesn't she know that people on there really aren't who they pretend to be? I've heard stories of stalkers and child porn…its people like that who are on the Internet. Freaks that can't function in the real world so they take refuge behind their keyboards and prey on unsuspecting innocent girls. I'm worried that she has grown men telling her stories. Maybe they can sweet-talk her into leaving me, too. I admonish her by saying "You realize you are really talking to fifty-year-old, bald, beer-gutted perverts, don't you!?" I worry about her, but I am to deep in my well of sadness to check more closely. She is a smart girl; I'm sure she will be all right.

I move from my chair to my bed. Now I don't even have to get dressed if I don't want to, and I also have another remote. I watch movies; I watch game shows, how-to's, nature series, comedies…just no sappy, crappy, bullshit romance stuff…who needs that!? Love…HA! Those movies just create false hopes and expectations of love that are far beyond my reach. None of that true love, happy ever after stuff ever really happens, so who needs exposure to it? Not me…I'm never going to believe in love again. It's all lies, just words…words…words…

There is a knock at my door. My daughter, Amber, wants to come in. "Sure honey, I'm awake…" sniff, sniff…

She lies on top of the covers next to me. She gives me a big hug…a hug from my baby; what a wonderful, heartwarming thing. I start to lose it and start crying profusely. " I can't keep going…I want to give up…I'm such a puss I just can't get over it!"

Amber laughs…I pull back. I look at her through my tear filled eyes; I wonder why she would laugh at me. "What are you laughing at?" I ask.

"You!" she replies.

"Why???" I insist on knowing.

Those deep blue eyes look at me, "Mom," she says, "You are the strongest person any of my friends and I know!!! And you are calling yourself a puss?!"

Again…I can laugh through tears, I tell her…"But I am a puss, I can't move on…I don't want to go on."

She pulls me closer and hugs me tighter; and begins to tap my back in much like the same way I would do to her when she was a baby. I start thinking back to how I was a child of barely seventeen when I had her and how she had caused me grow up so fast…yet I can't regret anything that allowed me to have her in my life. I am amazed at what an incredible person I have here next to me. "You will be fine…you've never needed him anyway, you've always taken care of everything," she tells me.

I ask her, "When did you get so smart? How can you know so much at fourteen?"

"Well, I am your daughter…I must have learned it from you!" she laughingly tells me.

What a butt kisser!!! I just love a kid who has enough sense to tell me what I want to hear when I need to hear it! I love that girl!!!

I'm really not alone. I keep my phone next to me all the time, and when I'm not calling a friend one of them is calling me. I just feel so guilty. When my life is clipping along fine, I sometimes go for months without calling any of my old school friends. Now when my life is a mess, I feel the need to call them over and over again to talk out all my horrible problems. Why they actually take time out of their busy lives to listen to my whining is unbelievable to me. I am so grateful to have all of them. I even get cards in the mail telling me that they are thinking of me and that they care about me. Phone conversations range from hang in there, maybe everything will still work out, to I always knew he wasn't good enough for you and that you deserved better but you were always so determined to work it out.

I had been determined, or—more honestly—stubborn. No matter how terrible things were, I would keep trying to make our marriage work out. I would change myself and anything else I possibly could to try and make Dickhead love me. Hmmm, when I think of it like that, it doesn't look so good. True, I always tried to change…but what did he do? Had his allowing me to change been his only contribution to the marriage? And why did I have to make him love me? Isn't that something he should have been able to do without any help from me? He originally was the one that chased me…he wanted me when I was sixteen, so why wouldn't he want me now? I'm the same person I've always been…I think.

I suffer from this horrible affliction called "alone". Sometimes it makes me crazy. I have to keep calling friends and relatives so that I have someone here with me. Amber is usually with me, but I need other adults to talk to. So even though I look like hell and never go out in public, part of me still has a desire to survive and overcome. Supportive friends and relatives have kept me from ending my existence and taking what I thought would be the easy way out. I still feel like the biggest fool on the planet, but maybe somehow I will someday be able to move on.

Amber has a boyfriend. This sweet kid has come along just in time to distract her from her problems and give her some happiness. I'm so excited that she has someone. I watch as he comes sheepishly to our door while she runs around like a maniac trying to look just the way she wants for him. I am happy for her. As she goes to run out the door, I holler at her, "Don't do anything I would have done! You don't want to end up like me, do you?"

"Don't worry mom, I'm not going to do anything that stupid!" she yells back at me.

"Well make sure you don't!" I tell her. I sure hope she doesn't. I have raised her to have a clearer sense of self than I ever did but I worry if now she will seek comfort in whatever way she can get it. I bite my lip, smile, and wave to them as they drive off. The most important part of me is now that young man's responsibility. I hope he realizes how important she is…how truly amazing that bubbly little blonde really is.

I get on the phone instantly and talk to friends about my day and my daughter's date. They listen intently and share with me parts of their days, things their children have done, and things they and their husbands plan on doing. I don't feel that I am quite as demanding on their time as I was the first week or so, but I do feel like I may be draining them. I call one after the other until Amber returns home. Here she comes, bouncing off the walls with excitement. How I envy her and her young love. I wish somehow I could feel that way again…someday. She shares with me all the details, and I hug her and congratulate her on her happiness. It is so incredible that she would share such things with me, her mother. After all, I would have never been so open and honest with my mother. I am grateful that we have been blessed with such a relationship. That honesty policy seems to be paying off!

~

Friday night, and Amber has agreed to go baby-sit for a friend of mine. She asked me first if I would be all right home by myself (being the little caretaker she is) and is now leaving me for the evening. I tell her I'm fine and I go to watch a movie in our living room. Finding that completely unsatisfying, I grab my phone and attempt to figure out whom I haven't bothered lately. I'm running out of friends fast, and the ones that I would like to call I know are busy off on family vacations tonight. What am I going to do?

I think of the computer and the Internet. I sit down and fire it up. I notice some news articles on the home page that look interesting. I haven't paid any attention to the rest of the world since mine collapsed. Well…it looks like the same old thing, so that's not very interesting. I continue scrolling around until I notice the top selections…travel, money, and weather—all sorts of choices, including chat. Chat…wasn't that what Amber used to spend all her time doing? I think I will just try that and see if I can find anyone to talk to.

I highlight chat and click my mouse button. My screen changes and a new display pops up. Go to a chat, start a chat, join a chat, pick a chat topic. Oh my, there seems to be a lot of options. I'm not sure what to do. I decide to look for a group of peers in some type of adult chat. Oh, wait…apparently I need a name. I'm not sure what to use. After some thought, I decide to use the name LonelyLady. It seems appropriate, considering my state of mind and present situation. I find a room called rendezvous. That sounds interesting…I highlight it and prepare to face…or not face…whomever. The words You are now chatting in rendezvous as LonelyLady appear on my screen. There are a list of names on the right of my screen, and rows of words moving on the left of my screen. Wow…I guess this is chat. I'm lost already. I'm trying to read what people have written as it zips past my viewing area. A differently colored set of words reads:

Bob whispers to LonelyLady: Hello, How are you tonight?

Oh no! I think he is talking to me! I wonder what I can do to reply? I type in, fine, and hit enter. I notice that my type wasn't colored like his was. I wonder why?

Bob whispers to LonelyLady: Do you want to whisper me?

Oh no…do I? How do I? I panic and hit something that sends me out of that chat. Now I don't know what to do. The chat is gone…where did it go? I think I would like to try that again. I grab my phone and dial the house where Amber is baby-sitting. She lets the machine pick it up. "Hello, Amber! This is mom please pick up the phone…I need you." She answers, concerned for my well-being. Once we've established that I'm fine, I ask her, "How do you get into those chat rooms once you get yourself out of that screen thingy that puts you in there?" I'm obviously completely puzzled.

"What are you trying to get in there for?" she laughs. "You want to talk to some fifty year old perverts or something?" she laughs harder.

"Just shushhhhh up and get me in there, smarty. You don't have to rub it in." I laugh back at her. Of course, I should have seen that coming after all the harassment I had put her through over this machine.

"Well you just go back to the home page and start over if you can't figure it out otherwise," she tells me mockingly.

"I'm not sure how to do that," I tell her. Then she proceeds to laugh and make fun of my limited computing skills. After about fifteen minutes of the Amber School of Computer Knowledge, I am back up and ready to go! "Thanks hun!!! You're brilliant!" I proudly state.

Okay…here I go again. Well where should I go? I scroll through a list that seems to have hundreds of different choices. "Love shack"? No. Bisexual-some-thing-or-other? I think I will pass. "Looking for friends" sounds too pitiful. Wow…look at all the choices! Religion, philosophy, art, music, teens, and on up to 50somethings…here is something—30s rooms! That would be me, although just barely. I am still just 31 (for a couple more weeks); anyway, I will try it. *Connecting*…and I'm in…again. After I'm in again, a few people type in Hello to LonelyLady after I've entered the chatroom. I move my mouse, get my cursor in that text box space and type in hello, then hit enter. Okay, this is easy. Now I've got it. I watch as conversations start flying past my screen again. *LOL, ty, wb* and a whole bunch of other stuff that makes no sense to me seems to make perfect sense to these other characters.

Back to Amber's School of Computer Knowledge. "What does LOL mean?" I question.

"Laughing Out Loud, or Lots Of Luck" she explains.

"Oh, thanks…that makes sense. How about ty or wb?" I ask again.

"Duh, Mother…it's Thank You and Welcome Back" she says, in a tone I now dread.

"Oh. Well, of course it is. I mean, I thought that's what it meant, but I just wanted to make sure," I try to say in a knowing motherly way. At the same time, I remember that this kid is very intelligent and it's probably due to the fact that I apparently passed any sense I had in my body through the umbilical cord.

Still laughing, she wants to know if I have any other questions. I don't…and I thank her again.

Ah, all right, then…let the chatting begin. Who do I want to talk to? Who would like to talk to me? I watch the screen for a while and fear that whoever did want to talk to me has since given up and moved on. I try to get into conversation:

LonelyLady says: 31/f/MN

I look at the screen and I see,

CutiePie says: 30/f/AZ
Hummer says: 35/m/CA
Crazylzzy says: 32/m/OH
Todd34 whispers to LonelyLady: Use your whisper button so we can talk

Okay…once again I have no idea what he is talking about. I look at my keyboard and can't find anything that says whisper button on it. I look at my screen and can't find anything that says whisper by it. I decide to be honest again,

LonelyLady says: what do you mean by whisper?
CutiePie says: Look over on the right part of your screen hun.
CutiePie says: You see those button shapes with the little symbols on it?

Okay now I feel like an idiot…they must all think I am an idiot.

LonelyLady says: yes I see them
CutiePie says: all right you just need to click on the one that looks like a bubble after you type somethin.
CutiePie says: oh but first you need to highlight the name of who you want to whisper to from that members list on the right of your screen
CutiePie says: do you see it?

I look all over my screen and see all kinds of things that make absolutely no sense to me. I see several buttons with different symbols on them. I see lots of different names. Oh, I see one of those slider bar thingies that let you look down on a list. I click on it and move it down. Cool, I see that Todd guys name…I move the mouse and click it. It changes color. Well there, that must have been what I was supposed to do. All right! Now I can type something. Wait…I can't find my cursor! Help! What did I screw up now? I slow down and think for a second. I take my mouse and move it to that type box again and click it. A-ha! There's a cursor again!! Now I am ready to chat!

LonelyLady whispers to Todd34: ok I think I've got it!
Todd34 whispers to LonelyLady: no problem hun what would you like to chat about
LonelyLady whispers to Todd34: I don't know I'm new at this

I'm so excited that someone else wants to talk to me that I can hardly stand it! A stranger wants to take the time to talk to *me*! How incredible, this might be fun after all!

Todd34 whispers to LonelyLady: what do you look like?

Oh no, I don't want to answer that. I look at myself and realize I haven't showered for two days and I look like hell. I quite possibly don't even smell very good…but then I remember hey, he doesn't know that.

LonelyLady whispers to Todd34: 5 foot 10, strawberry blonde with blue eyes, and what do you look like?
Todd34 whispers to LonelyLady: sounds nice! What are you wearing?

I figure he must not have read my question and I then look at myself. I didn't exactly dress for this occasion so I figure I will tell him the truth.

LonelyLady whispers to Todd34: blue jeans and a T-shirt
Todd34 whispers to LonelyLady: are your blue jeans tight?

All right…I don't know much, but to me this seems like an incredibly friendly conversation for someone I just met. I keep staring at the screen. Looking at his words that keep moving up the screen. I think to myself perhaps all conversations on the Internet start like this. Maybe I should just get with it and keep answering his questions.

Todd34 whispers to LonelyLady: hello are you still there?

Better yet, I decide to hit that little button again that causes me to leave the chat room. Whew…better to bail than to not know what to type. I regroup and decide to find another room. I start exploring some of the other room titles. There are so many to choose from, I don't know how people ever find their way around in this world. I enter one room after another, not really saying anything, just reading all the interesting nicknames. I notice some of these people are really creative and others are just plain nasty. I begin to wonder if I should change my name.

Lights flash across the back wall of my office. They startle me at first, and then I remember it must be Amber getting home from her baby-sitting job. I check the clock and to my surprise it is after 1 a.m. She enters the office and gives me that look…I'm not sure, but I think it was supposed to be a copy of that look that I always gave her when I felt that she was wasting her life away in this little room in front of this little box.

"Oh my god mom, you're still in the chat room?" Amber says with disgust.

"Well I'm just trying to figure out what it is that you are always doing in here," I say with purpose. I realize that she is too smart to fall for that line, but I'm giving it a shot anyway.

"Well, it was a long night and I'm going to bed. Try not to stay up all night, okay, mom?" she says, as she turns and heads off for bed.

"Hey, give me a hug first" I tell her, "I love you sweetheart!" I give her a big warm hug and she gives me one in return. I feel so lucky to have her. I will be all right…someday.

I return to my new discovery and continue meeting new people. I don't say too much because my typing skills are limited, but I at least get to talk to new people. I am fascinated by the fact that the people in these "rooms" come from all over the world, and yet are all in one space…sometimes sharing one conversation. I like it! I keep staring at my screen and adding to conversation whenever I get a chance. I notice lots of different code words and things I still don't understand. I stay at my post until my eyes can't focus anymore. I see that it is already 3 a.m., and decide to call it a night. I type goodbye to a couple of people that were talking to me, and reluctantly shut down the computer. I stumble up the steps and collapse into bed exhausted. I actually sleep…well.

LOL…My first attempt at a sexy pic.
I think that look suggests "terrified" more than sexy!

The sex instinct, which runs all through nature from the lowest animal to the highest, is the inborn impulse, craving or desire which one sex has for the other: the male for the female and the female for the male. This instinct, this desire for the opposite sex, which is born with us and which manifests itself at a very early age, is not anything to be ashamed of. There is nothing disgraceful, nothing sinful in it. It is a normal, natural, healthy instinct, implanted in us by nature for various reasons, and absolutely indispensable for the perpetuation of the race. If there were anything to be ashamed of, it would be the lack of this sex instinct, for without it the race would quickly die out.

It is necessary to impress this point, because many girls and women, whose minds have been perverted by a vicious so-called morality, worry themselves to illness, brood and become hypochondriac because they think they have committed a grievous sin in experiencing a desire for sexual relations or for the embrace of a certain man. Although it is necessary to impress upon the growing girl, when the occasion presents itself, that a thought or a feeling can never be sinful. An action may be, but a thought or a feeling cannot. Why? Because we are not responsible for our thoughts and feelings; they are not under our control. Though it does not mean that when they do arise we are to give them full sway. We should attempt to combat them and drive them away, but there is nothing to be ashamed of, because for their origin we are not responsible.

Woman: Her Sex and Love Life

To Boldly Go…

It was almost strange to wake up the next day wanting to get up, wanting to do something. That something was go online and chat…but…that had to be an improvement over wanting to stay in bed and hide from the world all day. I got up and logged on.

I spent the day exploring different chat rooms. Occasionally people were talking about religion, politics or world events; but more often it was stories about divorce and heartbreak. These strangers were all just as messed up as I was! Odd how comforting it is…being with your, "own kind". Hours flew by…I realized I didn't have my phone glued to my head. I thought about how relieved my friends must be to not have to deal with me today. They never made me feel like an imposition…but I still did. Even when they said they understood how I was feeling I knew they couldn't possibly. None of them were divorced. None of them had lived sixteen years for another just to have him cheat and leave…none of them…

Whewww…I look back up at my screen and realize I had just about closed myself off again. The curtains in my mind were just shutting out the light and the big heavy comforter was being pulled up to my chin. I shook off the feeling of utter loneliness and continued watching the chat conversations. Embarrassed by my lack of typing skills I didn't join in very often. I was enjoying just "listening" to everyone else for a change. I didn't always understand everything they were saying. It seemed that chatland had developed a bit of its own language. Single letters replaced some words, u=you, b=be, r=are, c=see, y=why and 2=too, 4=for and 8=ate…brb=be right back, omg=oh my god…ttyl=talk to ya later, okay was here simply—k.

My daughter still made fun of me spending so much time at this—waste of time—but she also saw me laughing and smiling like I hadn't done in weeks. It must have been a relief for her to have some time off from taking care of me. She was happy that I was feeling better…I was almost surprised to be…better.

Gradually I joined in more conversations and as my understanding of the chat language and my typing skills improved, I began to feel pretty social. Private whisper messages were returned with smiles ☺ and 32/f/mn, divorced, u? became just as natural as picking up a telephone and saying hello. Most of the time I found myself chatting with men but sometimes I'd come to the rescue of some helpless female newbie (chat for new to the net) and we'd share our life stories and tell each other to hang in there.

One evening while chatting a private message came in that caught my attention:

ManInBlack says: LonelyLady, I have one long deep passionate kiss to give you, where on your body would you like it?

I sat back in my chair staring at that sentence…and a new world opened before my eyes. Where would I like a kiss? Just the idea that I had a choice was new to me. I was not someone familiar with such choices…I mean sure, this was just online, but…still I have choices, I'm an adult. I was now for the first time in my thirty-two years a SINGLE adult, and I was on the verge of finding out just how many choices I really did have.

After the shock of the concept of choice settled into erotic interest I considered my options. One kiss, one passionate kiss, as my mind drifted I had a flash from the movie George Of The Jungle, where George says, "George have stirring of special feeling right now". I laugh to myself and proceed to drift off into a Brendan Fraser fantasy. Ahhh…okay…where was I? Focus, focus…oh yeah…someone wants to know where I would like a kiss. Hand, forehead, mouth, breast, clit…no I'd go with the kiss that makes me melt. The one that stirs my special feelings like a mixer set on puree.

LonelyLady says: I'd like that on my neck please.
ManInBlack says: Mmmm nice choice. I take you in my arms, run my fingers through your hair. You toss your head back and I trace my tongue along the edges of your face and proceed to give you the warmest most passionate kiss on your neck that you have ever had.

After I've read that I just close my eyes and let myself relax and feel what he has written. The neck was a good choice I think. I continued this first real attempt at cyber sex and enjoyed this man's efforts. For someone that was over a thousand miles away he was still the most attentive lover I had ever had. All through our online play as he shared all the other wonderful things he would do to me, he kept returning to my neck, to kiss the one place that he knew did something special for me. He remembered, this stranger remembered! I thought back to my now ex husband…I'd tried to train him for years to push my buttons, okay there was one that he figured out, but this passionate sensuous thing that I loved he had never seemed to care to hit. My mind wandered as the idea that other men could please me opened up a whole new path for me, one that excited me, one I needed to explore.

Girls of a highly sensitive or so-called "nervous" temperament, especially if there is "nervousness" in the family, must be particularly looked after. For it is during the years of puberty and adolescence that any neurotic traits are apt to develop and become emphasized. It is also the period when bad sexual habits (masturbation) are apt to develop, and the careful mother will devote special attention to her girls in their years of puberty, and guard them as much as possible against physical and emotional shocks.

Woman: Her Sex and Love Life

My New Family

Exploring my options online became a passion. I could always find someone to discuss whatever I had going through my mind. Happy days, sad days, lonely days…all were now better days, because of my peers online. Luckily one evening I stumbled across a group of thirty-somethings that would change my life forever. The chat room was called 30s5.

In case you have never been in a chat I will give you an example of what you could see. It's running multiple conversations scrolling from top of the screen to the bottom.
BTW, (by the way) this is where I learned that:

{{{{___}}}} = brackets mean hugs…and the more brackets the bigger the hug
LOL = Laughing Out Loud
LMAO = Laughing My Ass Off
ROFLMAO = Rolling On Floor Laughing My Ass Off…
And…when you're appalled you gasp, OMG (oh my gawd) and when you're pretending to be even more shocked—OMFG (oh my fucking gawd).

The following is a little sample of a CHAT:

Kitty says: dang I almost killed my puter with my bat!!!!!!
SisterMary says: hey I am gonna be a devil.. it is a stretch for me.. but.. I think I can pull it off.
Silly says: Crazy who will you be for halloween?? ☺

16

Anna says: lol Sister
Anna says: with a little padding and a wonderbra I should be able to pull off Elvira
Crazy says: mmmmm...taking suggestions
SisterMary says: LOL
Silly says: Sister my sister was a devil few years ago, lol that's one kinky costume lol
Silly will be a french maid this halloween
Crazy says: dictator
SisterMary says: hmmm maybe you should be the devil and me Elvira.. Anna
Anna says: good idea sister!
Kitty says: hey silly u'd better watch out though
Silly says: hey, why should I watch out??
Kitty says: cause I was a french maid a few yrs ago w net stockings
Silly says: kit.. and?? did you go trick or treating lol
StudMuffin says: Good Nite All...
Kitty says: and the guys wouldn't leave me alone
SisterMary says: Night Studly!
Anna says: Nite Stud
Crazy says: Love them net stockings.. mmmm
StudMuffin says: {{{{sistermary}}}}
Kitty says: night stuuuuudddddddd
StudMuffin says: gnite {{{anna}}}
Silly says: YUCK I hare net stockings
Girly says: nite nite studmuffin
Kitty says: hare????
Anna says: shave then philly
Crazy says: lol anna
Silly says: shave what????????? My legs????? LOL
Anna says: yes silly
Silly says: damn anna...I do wax all over
SisterMary says: well, I am going to bed...we rise early here at the convent
Anna says: nite sistermary
Anna says: nite roomies, I'm going to run too
Silly says: {{{{{{{{sister}}}}}}}} hugs night ☺
SisterMary says: good night everyone
Anna says: prayers with sister in the am
Crazy says: night anna smoooooch
SisterMary says: thanks for the cyber anna

Trip says: I rise early too sistermary...maybe we can work something out
Anna says: nite crazy, right back at ya babe
SisterMary says: LOL trip OMG
SisterMary says: wait can a sister say OMG???
Anna says: lol trip, try peeing.. hehehe that usually helps
SisterMary says: LOL night Everyone!
Kitty says: dang.. love you guys
SisterMary blesses kitty and her damn computer
Kitty says: meowing with laughter at sister!!!

There...that is chat. Not all chat...but, that was 30s5 chat. It was obvious this room was different. The people here seemed to know each other. They had some type of bond that interested me. I watched and eventually joined in...I introduced myself (after changing my nickname to Marie) and told them I hadn't been on chat long but was looking for some new friends. Everyone was so nice! Between talk in the room and private whispers, it was only a matter of days before I felt like I fit in.

SisterMary and I seemed to have very similar tastes in humor and cyber. I was amazed at her talent of simultaneous cybering. Men, I learned...are so easily entertained. You could tell them you were wearing anything...or nothing...and doing...whatever to yourself and they'd believe you. I played different scenes with different men. I learned what really pushed their buttons...and I had a blast poking at them. ;)

Some of us became so close it seemed the only way to keep up with everyone was to have a private community. The chat server allowed the creation of private web communities. A couple of the more computer literate brainiacs of 30s5 got the whole thing started. Someone would start a conversation by posting a Subject:_____ and then the other members could add their comments. Between the endless online conversations in chat and reading the postings on the community page...my life was full. I laughed everyday. I had people I cared about that cared about me. By just clicking and connecting...I could leave my small town life and the small town gossip and be part of new online gossip, LOL.

Bless my great friend Juliet for all her incredibly wise observations and conversations. She shared her strength, compassion, humor and understanding on numerous occasions and still does! I will share some actual community postings so you can see what witty wonderful women with the security of anonymity online will post.

Subject: A "Little" Story
From: Juliet
My best friend in the world and I met under strange circumstances...we were both boffing the same guy. I'm serious. He
introduced us. When a guy tells you that his ultimate fantasy is
having a "harem" of women who are all friends, the "DANGER"
sign should start flashing in your head...but when you are young
and foolish, you always believe the best in people.
Anyway, she and I had been acquaintances an actually had a good
bit in common. She came to visit me one night and as we sat
there chatting I said, "You know, I'm not sure if Paul is the greatest guy in the world or the biggest con man." She looked at me
with a shocked expression, said she had been thinking the exact
same thing, and that's when the proverbial shit hit the fan. The
bastard had actually been telling us the exact same lines...word
for word. I'd like to tell you that he had a redeeming quality but the
fact is we never found one. Despite his constant bragging, he was
a disappointing lover and well, shall we say, under-endowed. The
young woman and I however, became closer from the experience
becoming best of friends. We decided to room together the following year.
I bought her a housewarming gift for our new apartment. It was
the smallest cactus I'd ever seen. I handed her the gift and said,
"Here's your housewarming gift. I named him Paul...because he's
such a little prick."
We introduced "Paul" to everyone who came over that year,
spreading the...um, fame...of his predecessor far and wide. The
next time a woman comes to you with a broken heart because
some man or another has wronged her terribly...buy her a cactus...and name him accordingly.

I loved that story soooooooo much that I shared it with my local friends as
soon as the opportunity arose. I must have bought six cacti that week and sent
them along with little notes to friends. After Juliet posted her little story one of
the other community members posted his thoughts, and it snowballed from
there with different member adding their two cents (or more).

From: Max
Just a question here. But what do you do if it's a man in that situation? Does he buy his friend the oldest and biggest cat he can find and tell everyone about his old worn out big _____?

From: Lady
OMG, Juliet...I'm going out tomorrow to buy 2 cactus plants for my apartment...one will be named Keith and the other will be named Larry. Let's see...Keith was a big guy...better buy a big cactus and make him a big prick...LMAO. Larry was 5'9 and we did good to get him up to 130lbs. Better make him a little prick.
Oh, and Max...hon...I'll buy an itsy itsy bitsy one, and call it Max...ROFLMAO j/k
Luv yas! Lady

From: Juliet
Max...lmao...you are so nasty! But I love ya!

From: Anna
Juliet, loved the story—I laughed, I cried, the whole range of emotions. However, I have met so many pricks, no offense anyone, in my life that I don't feel a trip to the cactus store would help. I will definitely have to build a greenhouse where I will grow my own, each with their own little name. The biggest of all will be Ken, not because he was so well endowed, although he thought he was, but because he was indeed the biggest prick I have ever, or will ever meet. But that's another story. Anyway, thanks for welcoming me aboard. Look forward to sharing in the Community.

From: Marie
LMAO...MAX...U Funny!!! But I hate to think how many cats...you might have at your place...

From: John
ROFLMAO!!! makes u wonder........ I have 2 cats

From: Blondie
MAX! Look on the upside, or maybe it is the downside.........Cats have 9 lives!!!!!!

From: Erin

Anna, welcome to the community...

I did want to respond to your comment about Ken's delusion of being well endowed. The ladies have heard me say this before...They keep the delusion alive by brainwashing us that 3 inches is really 6 inches...

Okay ladies...I don't want to hear any snickering or comments about our instant message conference the other day...besides, I actually pulled out a ruler and discovered that I underestimated the measurements.

THANK GOD!!!

From: Blondie

Ladies!!!! And right now I am using that term loosely! That isn't exactly what I meant when I said people need to complete their "member" profiles!! If you don't knock it off, the guys are going to start demanding bra sizes!! Naughty naughty!

From: Marie

Let them ask...we don't care.. we will just lie.. like they always do...well, some of you can lie...I don't have too...:-P~~~~ just kidding!

Anyway...I absolutely LOVE the cactus story and have passed it on to my friends...OMG...just thinking about little pricks...cracks me up! TY for the smiles!

From: Robinhood

Dear Ladies of the Community,

Don't let any guy lie to you...when we were all in high school we measured them...Every guy does because he is pretty fascinated with this thing that pops up at the most inopportune moments. Like in the classroom at your desk and class ends and you hang out awhile...LOL but men do know although they may never admit it!

Damn I miss those crazies! I'll share one more community posting from Juliet. She wrote it after an evening of extremely entertaining group chat.

Subject: Hump Day in 30s5
From: Juliet
Last night was one of the funniest nights in chat history. So for those of you who missed it, here are the important things that we learned last night, in no particular order.

1. Chat and tape measures are a dangerous thing when mixed together.
2. Barb is a perv
3. Erin wears lacy green thong panties (we all checked)
4. Lucy's vibrating thingy is not big enough (that is a direct quote)
5. There is indeed such a thing as Dildo Insurance.
6. Robinhood is now known as Robinhood 7x2
7. Marie has a double headed dildo thingy (OMFG)
8. SisterMary gets none, but apparently has the most impressive collection of vibrating thingys...ahem...errr...amen?
9. Lysa has no vibrating thingys

And finally and most importantly the point that stood out most clearly from last night's chat is this...we all need extensive THERAPY!!! The first step is admitting you have a problem.

For I believe that wrong, perverted views of the physiology and hygiene of the sex act and of sex morality, that is, the proper relationship of the sexes, are responsible for untold misery, for incalculable suffering. Both sexes suffer, but the female sex suffers more. The woman always pays more. This is due to her natural disabilities (menstruation, pregnancy, lactation), to her age-long repression, to the fact that she must be sought but never seek.

Woman: Her Sex and Love Life

The Big Man

My chat family was my newly found salvation. Venting about my past experiences with others was helping me learn how to deal, and hearing others problems kept me compassionate. I did miss having a man I thought was special. I was a caretaker, a pleaser and a giver, I wanted a man in my life. Living in a rural area and knowing everyone's business makes the local men…less than favorable. Besides I wanted someone different. I began to search for him online.

There was a big man in the community that everyone seemed to like. He was single, funny and physically nothing like my ex. Six foot four about 260 pounds, with a shaved head, goatee and the darkest pair of mischievous eyes I'd ever hoped to look into. After a few private message sessions we spent time together on the phone. It made me very nervous at first, talking to a man other than my husband about all kinds of intimate details, but I enjoyed him. I invited him to my house for the weekend. When he agreed I almost backed out I was so nervous.

You need to remember that this was all new to me. I hadn't dated since I was sixteen, because that's when I met my first, who was also the man that I married. He was a skinny thing five feet and eleven inches and only about 150 pounds. The one my dad had told me to throw back because he was to small. Anyway…imagine my excitement over the six foot four man…mmm…I thought…this will be good.

He arrived late in the evening because it took a long drive to get to me. The first thing I saw was the reflection off the top of his head as it emerged from his car. Oh my gawwd I thought to myself what was I thinking! Then I opened the door for him let him in and he handed me a rose and gave me a simple sweet hug.

23

I had a hard time making eye contact with him as I led him into my living room. He sat in the chair and I on the couch. The silence was horrible. I was so uncomfortable yet he didn't appear to feel very out of place at all. I struggled with small talk. Then began to flip through the channels on the satellite dish until I found a movie he said he liked. A couple more minutes went by, although it seems liked hours, when he finally got more open.

"Didn't you tell me that if I came over we'd cuddle up on the couch together and watch movies?" he said with a smile.

Yikes I thought, now I have to touch this man! I tried to remain calm and replied, "Well of course we can", and with that I moved to the center of the couch.

So the big man got up and settled into the corner of the couch in a kind of sideways position and motioning for me to sit leaning up against him. I moved closer, positioning my back onto his stomach and my head on his chest. How wonderful I thought to have a man that I could actually cuddle into! He brought his long muscular arm down from the back of the couch and wrapped it around me. I may have shuddered a bit I'm not sure, but I know my heart was pounding a nervous beat not knowing what he expected of me or what his plans were. He carefully laid his hand on my arm. I eased up and settled into him a little more comfortably.

We watched the movie. We didn't speak much we just sat sharing the moment. Each of us enjoying having someone to hold. Someone to break the loneliness. I think it stayed like that for almost an hour. Then he lifted his hand from my arm. I began to get nervous again. Wondering what he was going to touch…wondering where he was thinking of placing his hand. Then with possibly the lightest most sensitive touch I had ever had…he pulled my hair back from my face. Softly tracing my temple and continuing to let my hair fall between his attentive yet coarse blue-collar finger tips. His soothing touch dissipated my nervousness and allowed me to meld into his form. I even got bold enough to begin to move one hand up and down his thigh, smiling as I considered all the other pleasures I may receive.

Eventually he traced down my jaw and tilted my head up toward his. He bent down and kissed my cheek lightly then he kissed my lips. I felt like it was my first kiss. I didn't even know how to return his kiss. Maybe I wasn't good at it I worried. I kept trying to think now…mouth open…maybe partly open…french maybe…???? Does he think or even realize how traumatic this is for me!!?? Yet the big man just remained calm holding me and kissing me softly not pushing not rushing just savoring and it gave me the opportunity to do the same.

I started realizing how uncomfortable it must be for him to be all bent over the way he was and I suggested we put some blankets down on the floor in front of the TV. He liked the idea and in no time there we were…in front of the television making out like a couple of kids. I had flashes to the time I was fifteen and grandma put me in charge of taking care of her house while she was away on vacation. It had been so convenient having a secluded private place to play with my then boyfriend. We'd spend hours just like this. Kissing by the light of the TV clothed yet exploring each other. My innocence intact, my heart racing, new feelings running rampant through my body, that's how I felt now.

As I lay on the blankets piled on the floor his kisses became more intense. My hands went to stroke his hair and then were surprised by the almost prickly new growth on his recently shaven scalp. This evening was full of new sensations. I had never even kissed a man with facial hair before it maybe wasn't what I had expected…or maybe it was…it's hard to decide. All I new was it was different, but different in a good way I was thinking.

His hands begin to wander, caressing and exploring my curves, I lay there enjoying, not questioning just accepting. He was content to just please me. It was a nice change for me. Not the typical…"Hey you wanna suck my cock?" foreplay that I had become sadly accustomed to during my married years. Apparently this man did find me attractive and was enjoying being with me…he kissed his way down my neck and began unbuttoning my blouse. I found myself just laying there watching him. His eyes seemed to light up a bit as my shirt fell open to my sides and he gazed at the black satin bra that was barely containing my ample breasts. While his left hand cupped one of the treasures he had discovered the right reached around behind me. He pulled me up off the floor and while kissing around my bra unhooked it in the back. He kissed my lips as he allowed me to lie back onto the floor while he carefully slipped the straps off my shoulders and then playfully tossed my bra across the room.

So there I lay…exposed, nervous, yet aroused and anxiously awaiting his next move. I could feel my nipples rising to meet his warm soft lips, I could feel myself ache for him in an area I had never shared with another man before. Yet I didn't want to share that yet I just wasn't ready. Luckily for me this man took his time. He spent hours kissing me, holding me, sucking and teasing my nipples, tickling me with his goatee, touching me…touch…something I had always craved and felt starved of…touches that came freely without expectations…touches that made me feel like a woman desired.

Occasionally as he kissed his way down my stomach he would pull at the button to my blue jeans…I would stop him and tell him I wasn't ready for that yet. He was a patient man. I think he knew it would pay off…(hahaha) so he let me pretend to be the frigid one. Strange thing was I surprised myself in how terrified I was at the option of having sex with this man. As I enjoyed his kissing, licking and teasing I tried to decide what I would let him do to me. I told myself...*you know sometime in your life you are going to have to be with a different man, and...why not get that scary part over*...I started to seriously consider letting this man please me in some of the other ways he wanted to. The next time he fumbled at the button to my jeans I didn't stop him.

He kissed my stomach while his hands rushed to pull my jeans off of my long legs. Then he sat up and pulled his own shirt off exposing his slightly hairy chest. I reached up and ran my fingers through it. It was another first of new sensations for me and I liked. I was so tempted to reach at his jeans and expose him further but I wanted to keep that a surprise yet. You know...like at Christmas when you have the biggest package under the tree and all your cousins are jealous because they know you are getting the best present...ohhhh yeah...that's what I knew I had to look forward to. And damn straight...although still being slightly shy and reserved...I was excited and looking forward to it! After all my ex was just a little man with about six and a half to pleasure with...this was bound to be a surprise that could possibly be overwhelming for me...but...no fear...game on.

The light of the television danced across my body while he hurried to slip off the black satin panties I had so carefully chosen shortly before he arrived. It made me a little nervous worrying about how wet I was afraid they had become thanks to his careful meticulous teasing. With the flick of a wrist they joined the heap of other discarded clothing...my blouse, bra, jeans, his shirt, and now my panties. Here I was with the worries of the old sin of nakedness running through my mind and yet...this man was telling me how beautiful I was and how much he wanted me. I considered stopping this whole episode but as his face reached the hot spot between my legs I decided to just let him enjoy himself awhile longer.

Wow, I thought, this is what has been terrifying me my whole life? Allowing myself some pleasure...what's so wrong with this? I decide to just quit worrying and delight in the pleasure I was receiving. The heat of his breath on my private place sent shivers up my spine. His tongue darted in and out of me as he suckled me. This really didn't seem so wrong...in fact, it seemed pretty right. After licking me into an almost entranced state he whispered that he wanted me. Rather than denying him I just uttered..."Bedroom...lets move to the bedroom."

I led him to the guest room where it was quite dark. Just a small amount of moonlight filtered in through the old lace curtains. I pulled back the blanket and laid down on the crisp clean sheets...it felt cold and I instinctively grabbed the blanket and covered up. I heard him fumble with his jeans and then I heard them thunk as they hit the floor. He pulled back the blanket and cuddled in close to me…feeling me shiver and realizing my nervousness he held me and kissed me softly. I tried to find the courage to let him continue his love making techniques on me. He asked if I wanted him inside of me and I told him I did.

As he slid his body over the top of mine I couldn't get over the size of the man. I liked the feeling of the weight of him on top of me. I liked feeling a little helpless…it excited me. He continued kissing me…I felt his underwear against my legs then he stopped to slide them off. I still didn't reach down to touch him…this was my biggest present ever and I was going for the greatest surprise of all. I couldn't believe what I was about to do. He stopped, kissed me, and made sure I was all right. I quietly told him I was fine and he continued his quest.

Now remember although I'd had sex regularly since I was just over 16 it had always been with the same man. I tensed as I could feel his manhood rubbing against my wetness. I was worried about what the shear size of this man would do to me. He moaned and so did I. Then my fear subsided into curiosity as I felt him enter me and then stop…he kissed me softly and pulled back out of my throbbing box. Then he entered again I waited for the big painful or possibly pleasure full feeling I was expecting. He pulled out again. *What the hell kind of technique is this?* I wondered. After a couple minutes of this game it started to get to me. *Why wouldn't he put it all the way in? What is he doing?* All legitimate thoughts wouldn't you say?

Well it occurred to me that since I hadn't touched it before hand…maybe he wanted me to play with it and stroke it a little bit. Maybe even ohhh and ahhh over the size or something…so I reached down. I reached down…grabbed a hold of his cock…and thinking I surely didn't have a good hold on it…gave it a little tug. Imagine my surprise when the little bugger barely crossed the palm of my hand! *What in the hell is that lil thing doing there?* I was astonished. All that waiting for my big package and it was like the year I just got a blanket! I didn't want a damn blanket!!! I wanted a TOY!! I wanted a BIG TOY!!!!…

WWAAAHHHHHHH…I felt like crying. All hopes were bashed.

I stroked him for a minute and then squeezed out a hopefully pleasant moan and let him finish what he had started. After he came he kissed me and asked, "Was I big enough for you?"

Thank goodness it was dark in the room so he couldn't see me biting my lip while I responded, "Of course you were, why would you ask that?"

You know…I bet I had almost the same dumb founded look on my face that Christmas after opening my big present and I had to smile at the blanket and then at my auntie and tell her, "Why thank you! Its just what I needed."

I had an epiphany that day. Always check the package…shake it, jostle it, rub it a little…look under the wrapping a little maybe…but…always check the package. If I'd only had some idea before hand I wouldn't have been so disappointed! I'm also sure that a short-peckered man started that nasty, size doesn't matter, rumor too.

My Favorite Cock

Chapter Forty-Three (Woman: Her Sex and Love Life)
Advice to Frigid Women, Particularly Wives

I wish to give you a piece of advice which is of extremely great importance to you. I hesitated somewhat before writing this chapter, but the welfare of so many women depends upon following this advice, and I have seen the lives of so many wives spoiled on account of not having followed it, that I decided to devote a few words to the subject.

As you know, about one-third or one-quarter of all women (in other words, one out of every three or four) are sexually frigid. They either have little or no sexual desire, or if they do have, they experience no voluptuous sensation during the act, and never have an orgasm. If you are unmarried, well and good. But if you are married and happen to belong to the frigid type, then *don't inform your husband of the fact*. It may lead to great and permanent trouble. Some husbands don't care. Some are even glad if their wives are frigid. They can then consult their own wishes in the matter, they can have intercourse whenever they want and *the way they want*. They do not have to accommodate themselves to their wives' ways, they do not have to prolong the act until she gets the orgasm, etc. In short, some husbands consider a frigid wife a blessing a God-sent treasure. But, as I mentioned several times before, in sexual matters every man is a law unto himself, and some men feel extremely bad and displeased when they find out that their wives have "no feeling." Some become furious, some disgusted. Some lose all pleasure in intercourse, and some claim to be unable to have intercourse with any woman who is not properly responsive. Some begin to go to other women, while some threaten or demand a divorce (of course, such men cannot really love their wives; they may use their wives' frigidity as an excuse to get rid of them).

Now, a man has no way of knowing whether a woman has a feeling during the act or not, whether or no she enjoys it, whether or no she has an orgasm. These are subjective feelings, and the man cannot know them unless you tell him. If you belong to the independent kind, if you scorn simulation and deceit, if, as the price of being perfectly truthful, you are willing if necessary to part with your husband or give him a divorce, well and good. You are a free human being, and nobody has a right to tell you what to do with your body. But if you care for your husband, if you care for your home and perhaps children, and do not want any disruption, then the only thing for you to do is not to apprise your husband of your frigid condition. And it won't hurt you to simulate a feeling which you do not experience, and even to imitate an orgasm. He won't be any wiser, he will enjoy you more, and nobody will be injured by your little deception, which is after all a species of white lie, and is nobody's business but your own. An innocent deception which hurts nobody, but, on the contrary, benefits all concerned, is perfectly permissible.

It may seem rather strange publicly to give advice to deceive and to simulate. And it is undoubtedly the first time that this advice has been given in print. But as I have only one religion-the greatest happiness of the greatest number-I repeat that I can see nothing wrong in advising something which benefits everybody (concerned) and hurts nobody. More than one household which was threatened with disruption was preserved safe and sound by a little simple advice which I gave to the wife, without the husband's knowledge. He was satisfied, and things after that ran smoothly.

Some women are afraid to simulate a voluptuous or orgastic feeling, because they think the husband can discover whether their feeling is genuine or they are only simulating. (Women, and men too, have funny ideas on sexual subjects). This is not so. A notorious demimondaine, who was greatly sought because she was known to be so "passionate," confessed that not once in her life did she enjoy intercourse or experience and orgasm. But her mother, who also suffered with absolute frigidity, taught her to simulate passion, telling her that in that way she could make barrels of money; which she did.

It is deplorable that wives or husbands should ever be obliged to have recourse to deception or simulation; perfect frankness should be the ideal to be striven after. But under our present social conditions and with the present moral code, an occasional white lie is the lesser of two evils; it may be the least of a dozen evils.

Woman: Her Sex and Love Life

Everything's Plucky

I had learned the lesson: All men are NOT created equal. Yet it seemed a cruel thing to not see someone again because of something they couldn't exactly change. So I did see him again. The next time I drove to his home. He was a kind host and a good cook. It was so nice to have someone that fussed over me! Dinner by the television…but dinner he had cooked and served to me ☺ I decided to over look his…umm…shortcomings and someday introduce him to an extension.

One day while chatting with him online I grabbed some paper when I started feeling poetic. I wanted to write something about taking a chance on love. This is what I wrote:

Tempted
As letters flow across my screen,
My heart begins to beat again.
What is that heart? You still exist?
I thought that pain had ended this,
This hope to find a caring soul,
That once I find would make me whole.
Who is this man that I can't see
Whose words so sweet just tempted me,
Just tempted me to live again,
May he be lover…or kind friend.

We spent more time together and played out some public fantasies like sex in a theater on a Sunday afternoon. I picked which movie based on the fact that "Pee Wee Herman" was one of the actors and after what he went through, the two of us having sex (in front) of him was just to funny and ironic. My ex would have to be forced just to have his arm around me in a theater. How naughty, how risky…how I wished Dickhead knew how easily I had moved on. The big man and I test drove sports cars pretending to be in the market…and went ninety miles an hour through the city streets. He took me to comedy clubs; we went dancing…he had the DJ play a special song for us. I met his children; I met his parents…I thought how lucky I was to find someone that really liked me the first time out. I wouldn't have to be alone. I'd found someone.

Forget that he had no money. Forget that he couldn't make me climax. Forget that he seemed to have stopped trying. Forget that he lived four hundred miles away in a small house with a yard that wouldn't support one of my horses much less thirty of them. He liked me. I was lucky.

One night on the phone with him I got a bad feeling. I asked him if he still wanted to see me and if he was coming to my place that coming weekend. He started to tell me he wasn't sure yet if he could. Something else was maybe happening…blah, blah, blah…I pushed him and asked what was wrong. At first he said nothing was wrong but I couldn't be satisfied with that. I had to keep pushing. He admitted that he was interested in someone else and that we were not going to work out. I was crushed. I was wounded. I was dumped again…what the fuck was wrong with me, I wondered.

Immediately I went to my chat home. I found my girlfriends and cried my sorry tale to them. Than I went to the community pages and told everyone what a short-peckered, lying bastard their friend Rooster was. I wanted to make him pay, I wanted to make him hurt. I wanted to ruin his status in the community as a good man and a great dad. Some of my new female friends had been friends with him months before I came along. They chewed his ass in private messages and saved them and sent them to me. He told them he cared about me and liked me, and that I was fun, but it just wasn't going to work out. They told him to tell me that. He sent me a card:

I'm sorry things turned out this way. I feel bad for hurting you. I was thoughtless. Please forgive me if you can.

—P

He posted in the community sight:

Subject: an apology
From: Rooster
Dear friends,
I humbly stand before you to apologize for being careless with certain people's feelings. I beg for your forgiveness. I broke one of my own rules: don't be careless with others' hearts, you wouldn't want them to be careless with yours. I may not be around the chatroom much, because I am ashamed of what I have done. I won't be careless anymore.
Again, I am truly sorry. Please forgive me—Rooster

I let other members of the group respond to him without saying anything myself. Juliet, Lady and Kitty all left kind words about being glad he was man enough to apologize and that they would continue to be his friend if he straightened himself out. A week later I posted a response.

From: Marie
Ok...I have waited to answer to this until my heart could let my head do the talking...
I have met some incredible people here and I cherish every one of them. You however were allowed to share more than that with me...which I am not regretting. I had more fun with you over a couple of weekends than I have had over the last several years put together.(sad but true) What really hurt was the fact that you couldn't be open about your feelings...whatever happens from here on out...please talk things through...this room is really no longer just a play land...it's a group of friends that are more like a family...and you know how special family can be. Take care, stay kind, be open...Marie

I stay up late talking with friends. I cried over not being the right one for him...I cried over worrying about not being the right one for anyone. I cried over letting myself get hurt again. My daughter came into my office and wrapped her arms around me and told me she loved me. I had her sit on my lap so I could just hold her and feel comforted. I was lucky to have her with me.

I went to bed. I grabbed a piece of paper and scribbled down this poem before I went to sleep. 3:45am.

I laughed, I smiled...
I enjoyed life...once again.
I took his hand in mine.
I let him in close,
I shared myself with him.
For what? Is this life?
I took a bite out of life,
Not even considering
Poisons pain...
I cried, but I lived.

The hygiene of menstruation can be expressed in two words: cleanliness and rest. Common sense would suggest these two measures, and as far as rest is concerned, many women do rest or take it easy while they are unwell.

It is an outrage that many delicate, weak girls and women must stay on their feet all day or work on a machine when they should be at home in bed or lying down on a couch. It is not necessary that work be given up altogether, but there certainly should be less of it and there should be as much rest as possible. For delicate and sensitive girls it is always best to stay away from school during the first and second days.

Woman: Her Sex and Love Life

"Ladies" of Chat

Marie: Hi! What are you still doing here???
Blondie: brb, need some advil, I have a fever
Marie: ok sorry to hear that
Blondie: Hey, I whispered this fun guy last night, got his pic and...nope ain't gonna happen, he wants me to go to Cleveland.
Marie: Auugghhh...not you too, why do we find men that want us to do the traveling.
Blondie: I swear, I'm not going to see anyone, they have to come see me
Marie: True, or at least pay for the damn ticket to get us there!
Blondie: Good thinking, no more poor guys!!!
Marie: Damn right, why do I always pick the broke ones?
Blondie: It's because tough guys make fun dates and I always think they will be more attentive in bed
Marie: didn't you just see...ummm...what's his name, and doesn't he have money and some talent???
Blondie: Yes, and he (Samuel) is off to Canada to meet some girl (since we're just "friends"), but I don't know if he went or not, we are suppose to get together and hang out on Sunday night. Dang, this is too complicated, I think I'm getting in over my head.
Marie: hmmm...very interesting though

Blondie: yes, it is...just refuse to analyze it. Hey, I am getting good at this flirting thing
Marie: woohooooo, practice, practice, practice...isn't it fun!!! Here read this:
> Marie Whispers to BigJimmy: lol, at your nic hun...but, it does give me hope! ☺
> BigJimmy Whispers to Marie: I'm Italian, 42, 5'8, 150#, slender, 33 waist
> Marie Whispers to BigJimmy: hey bigjimmy, damn it, I'm bigger than you! I HATE that.
Blondie: OMG soooooo funny. FRESH MEAT, FRESH MEAT
Marie: lol, and I was going to go out tonight
Blondie: This is one of those really good nights with lots of people online
Marie: guess my ass is planted here for the night...again
Blondie: Incoming cut & paste!!!
> BigJimmy Whispers to Blondie: Blondie you are very attractive with lovely legs and breasts.
Marie: LOL...that's the shortie!!
Blondie: GET SHORTY!!
> BigJimmy Whisperes to Blondie: you can keep on flirting, do you mind that I'm here nude
Marie: eeeeeeeeewwwwwwwwwwwwwwww
Blondie: Just trying to get you some material, lol
Marie: lol, thanks ;-)
> Blondie Whispers to BigJimmy: OMG don't tell me that
> BigJimmy Whispers to Blondie: you can't be a virgin
Marie: fuck...I have 6 regulars on...all right NOW, DAMN!
Blondie: regulars? Now you do sound like a hoe! J/k ;-)
Marie: I am...
Blondie: nah, you're just pretending, and taking revenge on the hubby
Marie: okay, true...you're good
Blondie: yup, been there and done that, that's how I landed hubby #2 unfortunately
Marie: well I am fishin in a damn big pond
Blondie: just be smart, this is safer than doing it in real life
Marie: yesssssssss
Marie: btw, when you're cybering more than one at a time, always answer yes to this question.

Riker Whispers to Marie: are you typing one handed?
Blondie: OMG!!!
Marie: LOL, then you can jump around and do more than one, and they think you are really getting off...hehehe
Blondie: thanks for the tip!
Marie: I had to go look at Sam's pics again, that smile...yummmmm! And now all I can think is...
Blondies had that!
Blondie: I wonder who is having him tonight
Marie: Do you care?
Blondie: Damn it, yes I think I do. I don't want to care, I'm trying not to
Marie: WOW, he must have been good
Blondie: He says the sweetest things and than contradicts himself all the time
Marie: LOL
Blondie: We are supposed to meet up tomorrow night
Marie: Are you nervous?
Blondie: No, I enjoy his company. We have been out about 7 times or so
Marie: you need to remember there are other penis's out there
Blondie: he says we are just friends that say the word date and all this other stuff than he asks me how I like to decorate, do I want kids, what kind of house do I want and all that stuff.
Marie: he is confused...do you want kids?
Blondie: with the right person. Do you thinks that's it, he is just confused?
Marie: of course he is, all men are
Blondie: oh great, the woman he was going to meet just showed up online
Marie:?????
Blondie: well it is 1am and she is married, maybe they just met up
Marie: she's married??? Omg, Samuel is a dog...RUN
Blondie: supposedly she wants to leave her husband
Marie: blah, blah, blah...we've heard it all before
Blondie: hmmmmmmm, guess I find out tomorrow. I told him I was meeting people too sooooooooo, what is fair is fair, or are we both just playing it cool
Marie: good luck! ☺

Blondie: Damn, I should have never done this, why is my stomach in my shoes
Marie: Damn, you care…amazing isn't it!
Blondie: yes, and I don't like the way it feels one bit!!!
Marie: ohhh you'll be ok, it could be great yet
Blondie: I think I will just turn off my brain, or try too
Marie: want me to ask her where she's been all day?
Blondie: no, might be to obvious
Marie: where were they going to meet?
Blondie: Niagara Falls
Marie: how could she pull that over on her hubby?
Blondie: she told him they were more like roommates now
Marie: omg, how many times have you heard that here???
Blondie: really, Christ I broke my rule. He says his rule is never to fall for someone he meets on the internet
Marie: shame on you, I would never do that…more than…6, 7, 8 or so times
Blondie: OMG, guess it is my turn, they call these guys transition men
Marie: so…fuck em
Blondie: yup, and than…fuck em again!

The following is an email from my sweet friend Blondie:

Subject: Diary of a Divorcee

Stayed in bed all morning just to pass the time,
There's something wrong here, there can be no denying….
It's 1:30pm and I just now got out of bed. Granted, I did stay up until 2 something last night, but still shouldn't have slept this long. Woke up periodically throughout the morning, but could think of no reason to get out of bed. Then it dawned on me "I've got laundry in the dryer, if I don't get it folded, those wrinkle-free pants will be wrinkled" Discovered there is no such thing as wrinkle-free pants.
I have absolutely no reason to get up…no one to take care of (no one to take care of me either), no boss to report to. Suppose I could cross-stitch, but don't seem to have the energy lately to pick up a needle and canvas. My hair looks like shit. Should take a shower and get dressed, but hell, who is going to see me? My aunt, possibly, as I wander aimlessly about the house, stepping outside now and then for a smoke or heading to my room a zillion times a day to check my email?

Today I am avoiding my cell phone because I have again given my number out to someone I have no intention of starting a relationship with. Damn, I have got to stop doing that. It's not fair to the other person. Someone out there might actually be getting excited at the thought of getting to know me. I don't want to go through that getting to know someone stage. I want to go immediately to comfortable and settled. What the hell am I doing? Had 5 guys going last night, and received emails from another 3 this morning that I haven't spoken to in a while. This is not a good thing.

Have to get in the shower, have to get dressed, have to do something productive, because if I don't attempt to do this everyday, the day will come when I just won't bother to get up at all. Then the days ill turn into weeks and eventually the men in white coats will come get me with that big white net and haul me away. Not a bad idea if I had some insurance and could go to one of those really nice places with tennis courts and a golf course!

Ok, here I go…I'm going to go get ready…for absolutely nothing and nobody. Hey I am somebody. I will get ready for me. That is something I keep telling myself…it doesn't work so well anymore.

Sorry about that Marie, I try not to do that too often for fear of sinking lower and lower, but just had to get it out. And to be frank, that is the most brutally honest I have been about my feelings…I don't even tell my shrink this stuff. Had to get it out today…and what the hell…it sounded great for the book!

<hugs> Blondie

I had shared with my online girlfriends my hopes of someday writing a book about my experiences. They were kind enough to share some of their most intimate writings. Too often women seem to feel alone. We need to remember to be honest with each other and realize no matter how we attempt to portray ourselves to the world deep down we are so much the same. The next piece was written by my friend Juliet when she realized her romance with someone states away was never going to be her reality.

Subject: Au revoir

Well, I guess that is the crux of it isn't it. I am not, nor have I ever been as impor-tant to you as you made yourself to me. While you were flirting and having fun and "not taking things too seriously" I was thanking God that it seemed as if finally at last, here was someone worth my time, my energy, my effort. Here was someone worth losing sleep over. I only wish you felt the same way about me.

It isn't a surprise by now and your letter only stings a little, the pain of losing you has been ebbing away slowly. I didn't lose you all at once; it happened piece by piece like someone carving out sections of my heart. First the birthday forgotten, the pictures and cards never sent, all the little things you wouldn't find the time to do for me. When I called you on it, you wrote a heart wrenching poem for me implying that your feelings for me were much deeper than "just having fun". I was touched though still upset. I thought hmmm maybe I have read him all wrong, maybe he didn't lead me on, maybe he really does have deeper feelings for me. So I held on. And even with that first slice gone, I let myself believe, believe in myself and my instincts, believe in you. I tried in every way to be loving and supportive. Then the infrequent calls, the falling off of the emails etc. and every time another piece.

I wish you the best of luck Tony. I am not angry. I pity you too much for that; not for all the things that are happening to you but for what you do to yourself. I am a wonderful woman that you will not let yourself care about, not really, not fully, not in any way that is meaningful. You say you want certain things in your life but when someone comes along who just might want to and be able to give you those things, not to mention make you truly happy, you push her away when you need her the most. I find it ironic that in your "Dominion of Loss" poem you accuse me of chasing the sun when as it turns out you are the on who wanted only the light. I am disappointed in you; I am disappointed in me. I let myself believe in the magic of that voice on the line. I should have known better, should have gone with my head instead of my heart. I wish I had that luxury. I wish I could just shut everyone out sometimes too. I guess this is the price of my passionate heart.

I am more than capable of understanding that you "have so much going on" I have been through some very dark times myself. I also know that it takes about 15 seconds to send an email saying "Things are crazy here but I am thinking of you and will be in touch when I can." I am sorry that your life is full of so much pain right now. I know it is exhausting. But I also know that when people are important to you, you find a way to let them know it. And more importantly, I know that in the darkest times in my life it was the love and understanding of my friends that got me through it. If you push and push and push people away eventually you'll wind up alone in the middle of nowhere.

I am glad that you think the time we spent together worthwhile. Myself if I had seen this coming, would have gone to bed earlier on more than one of those long chatting nights. You are a wonderful guy but I thought we were building something not just playing around. You were the one who responded to my comment that this whole thing was crazy with reassurances about flights, and phone calls, and how things can work. I really believed that we'd meet, see if the chemistry was there in person, and take this thing for a test drive. I didn't realize that this was just entertainment. I really believed that we had grown close, that you would turn to me when times were tough. I would have liked to have been "the calm you seek".

No wonder I have been confused. I apologize for misinterpreting; you must think me silly.

I never wanted or needed perfection. As Billy Joel sang, "You've given me the best of you, now I need the rest of you". I never realized that you never intended for me to have more than the flirtatious side of you. I guess you enjoyed being a knight in shining armor. Maybe you still do...

I understand that living with Jill and the gang has put some restraints on your time but I also know that were the situations reversed I would have found a way to spend time with you. It would have been important enough to me to find a way. There is always a way to work things out if it is worth the effort.

Sorry you didn't like Len's poem. I love it. All of his work really. It is edgy and sometimes dark but it is brimming full of real life and real emotion. I suppose that one struck me most of all given my current situation and maybe that is why I sent it. I didn't think of it as "attacking" as much as "thought provoking" but I guess we all see things according to our mood and frame of reference. Wonder why you felt attacked by it? You are right; I probably shouldn't have bothered. I probably shouldn't have bothered with any of this over the last four months and saved time, energy and money. Hope is a beguiling thing. I believed that you were worth it.

Remember this, "I thought we were on the same page when it came to acknowledging that we were friends. It was fun to be flirtatious and have someone to talk to. I thought neither one of us was taking things too seriously". You suck. Period. End of story. ARE you KIDDING ME??????????????? Oh I want you to come see me, want to come see you, want to be loving and supporting, want you to understand me. Was it fun being someone's fantasy? Must be quite the power trip. Did you enjoy all the little things you did to make yourself indispensable? Did you get off knowing that a poor lonely woman thought you were the answer to a prayer? I'm glad one of us enjoyed it. I can't believe the ways I opened myself up to you and now to discover that it was all fun? That it was all flirtation? That I was ENTERTAINMENT? You jackass, you even told me you loved me first! I was really trying hard to NOT go there. Then it came whispered late in the night, and fool that I was, I let myself believe it.

Many of us are on the internet because we are having a hard time trusting again, diving into real life relationships. Unfortunately, trusting people you meet in this box only leads to more heartache. I hope that I am strong enough to face this without regressing. I am going to try like hell to not give you that power. And you know what, I think I can do it. I thought you were different from these other internet guys who are too afraid of having real relationships so they play at it on the net. I guess I was wrong. You were careless with my heart; and that was really wrong. I

hope that in seeing the pain I feel coming through this letter you will at least have the decency to avoid doing it to someone else in the future.
Don't worry about me sending you anything. I regret the time and effort I have spent already and I am not going to invest anything more. This is my last email before I delete you from my list and my life. I hope that you someday realize that playing at being what someone wants and needs isn't playing at all. Good luck with your life. You will one day realize what you let get away. I could have been that missing piece that helped your life come together, only you were to closed off to let it happen. Goodbye Tony, thanks for the poems and for the fantasy. I wish I wasn't naïve enough to still believe that dreams can come true.

*   *   *   *   *

I really enjoyed having "new" female friends. It's hard to live in a small rural area and have any opportunity to meet new people. I could connect online and meet a new person every second of everyday if I wanted to. When the Rooster episode was coming to a close three of the women from the 30s5 chat room were planning on spending a weekend together. When I asked if they would mind me crashing their party they welcomed me with excited emails.

From: Blondie
To: Marie, Silly & Juliet
Subject: Girls Weekend
Date: Monday, September, 13

Hi Marie, Silly & Juliet!
I'm attaching my phone numbers in case anyone needs to reach me. I will be in the Long Island office Friday until about 3pm. Let's just hope that that hurricane Floyd stays out of our way. Just like a man to try to screw up our plans. Weatherman says the East Coast might get hit with hurricane force winds on Friday.
Marie, I will probably look like a slob when I pick you up. Prefer to wear traveling clothes, especially if the weather is bad.
Can't wait to see you all, my therapist is now totally convinced I am a nut! Actually she thinks this is really great.
Love,
Blondie

From: Marie
To: Blondie, Silly & Juliet
Subject: Re: This Weekend!
Date: Tuesday

Okay Everyone...
I am so excited about this weekend! I have never just hopped on a plane and done something for me...this is sooo cool. Unfortunately, well not really, but I spent all my extra cash stash on four new horses yesterday! So, I won't be able to blow too much money. We will have to work on free drinks, LOL...WOOHOO, I am sooo excited, did I type that already?!
Oh, BTW, this flying to meet strangers from the Internet thing, still has some of my friends freaked out. The last comment was, "I hope you don't get off the plane and find out they are all lesbians...you don't need that." LMAO!! Can you believe that?! Well I sure hope that everything works out with the weather and all of your schedules. What should I bring? What should I wear? Etc...write and tell me!
Marie

From: Silly
To: Marie, Blondie & Juliet
Subject: Lezbi Friends
Date: Tuesday

Oh my gosh Marie one thing I know for sure is that I am no lezb-ifriend, LOL.
Marie, bring along something casual as well as dressy, after all you will be here all weekend, you never know where you will go or who you will meet ;-)
On Sunday I hope we will all be casual, after Saturday night I don't know what condition I will be in LOL.
Can't wait to meet you all, Luv you,
Silly

From: Juliet
To: Marie, Blondie & Silly
Subject: Girls Weekend
Date: Thursday

Hey Girls!
As long as Floyd doesn't screw everything up we are going to have
a ROCKIN WEEKEND!
Itinerary:
Friday night: Arrive, settle in, freshen up, then out to either the
Big Kahuna (David Lee Roth is there) or into Downtown
Wilmington to do the bar scene.
Saturday Day: possibilities—Cow Town flea market—always an
adventure, Lancaster outlets-shopping & we can see some
Amish, Baltimore Inner Harbor—all kinds of cool stuff Nat'l
Aquarium, etc.
Saturday Night: Ladies night, get dolled up and head to Phila to hit
the club scene
Sunday: We'll decide if we survive till than!
Well gals, I'll talk to you soon. I can't wait to see you! This is SO
awesome!
Love ya,
Juliet

From: Blondie
To: Marie, Silly & Juliet
Subject: Friday
Date: Thursday

Marie,
As it stands right now, the three of us will meet you at the air-
port!!! Isn't that cool, or maybe a little nerve racking! OMG to step
off of a plane to see the three of us. Hope you don't turn around
and get right back on the plane. The weather should be fine, but
we are all going to call TWA to check on your flight.
If I don't catch any of you online tonight, I will SEE you in 27 hours!
I am really looking forward to this. Love yas,
Blondie
PS. I think we should call Oprah!

From: Blondie
To: Marie, Juliet & Silly
Subject: Today's THE Day
Date: Friday

Hi, Hi, Hi!
It's 7:21 Friday morning. The sun is shining, the wind is dying down, and it is absolutely beautiful. Marie, you should have no problem flying in! I got moofed again last night and then my cable modem crapped out. What a night for that to happen. That's ok though, cause I really had to pack. By the way, I have a blow dryer packed!
OMG OMG OMG OMG How will I ever concentrate at work!
Blondie

From: Marie
To: Juliet, Silly & Blondie
Subject: WOOHOO
Date: Friday

Okay ladies, I can hardly stand it!
If I survive getting to all of you I am going to have a great time! I hope you are all in the mood to have some fun, I NEED to have some fun!
I have Blondie & Silly's cell phone numbers if I'm delayed or have any trouble. Once again I will be on TWA flight 552 Minneapolis to St. Louis, then flight 710 St. Louis to Philadelphia!!! Hmm, hope I get lucky and meet some handsome hunk on the plane ☺
I'm having a hell of a time deciding what to pack. I asked for Webby's advice and he said, "Condoms dear, lots of condoms," LMAO...what a man.
See You ALL Soon
MarieIsSoExcitedSheCanHardlyWait

This adventure was honestly one of the most exciting things I had ever attempted. I made arrangements for Amber to stay with her godmother and my brother was going to feed my critters and watch my place. Everyone on my messenger friend's list was aware of my big plans and thought it was pretty cool to meet online friends in person. Many of my IRL (In Real Life) friends thought I was crazy and worried about my safety. Most of my local friends would never jet off spur of the moment just for a party weekend, especially not alone.

My heart raced faster than my Dodge on the way to the airport. I had known these women less than three months but we shared more in those months than I'd shared with anyone else my entire life. We'd seen just a couple photos of each other, however this wasn't any type of romantic weekend between us and the pressure was off for impressing anyone. It was so much better than stressful predate preparations, yet I wanted these women to like me and I hoped that face-to-face I'd live up to my online persona.

I'm not sure if I was verifying the incredible lack of leg room in the plane or if I was just sitting so incredibly upright that I could actually see my feet, but I remember when the plane took off and I got that—lighter than air anything is possible—rush. I was doing something just for ME. I was on my way to see MY friends. As distraught as I'd been when Dickhead turned my life upside down I now felt at ease. Much more so than the poor flight phobic gentleman sitting next to me doing some hypnotic deep breathing exercises with his eyes sealed shut while quashing my hope of chatting with someone sexy on the plane.

When I walked off the plane I tried to hide my nervousness behind a smile and a confident stride. I searched the crowd and there they were…three thirty-something women bursting out of themselves with excitement. We exchanged hugs and none of them groped my ass or tweaked a boob. I made a mental note to inform my homophobic friend back home. Instantly we were chatting away like we'd known each other forever, without awkwardness like I'd expected.

The weekend went great with some of the highlights being: a minor fender bender before we left airport parking, an incredible meal at an open air Italian Restaurant in a historic part of Philadelphia, dancing with a couple short Asian men after downing Blondie's favorite mind altering drug—Rumple Minze (100 Proof Schnapps), and some slightly fuzzy memories of a couple guys at a sports bar in Delaware—where I learned the reason so many women go to the bathroom together—so the guy you were hitting on doesn't hit on your friend while you're busy peeing. Even when I've been drinking I am capable of noticing when the man whose hand is on my ass has his other hand on my friend's ass. Juliet and I had a small conference about that fact when he went to pee and we decided to just play that out a little longer.

Silly had a husband and had to go home. Blondie, Juliet and I let the ass grabber and his friend follow us back to Juliet's apartment. While Juliet was busy being the hostess I was out on the patio making out with the ass grabber. Then when Juliet needed to take her dog out to pee Mr. Assgrabber graciously offered to help. Blondie was busy almost flirting with assgrabber's friend, or at least until she starting speaking to Ralph on the big white phone. When Juliet returned she pulled me aside to talk to her.

"When you were out on the patio together was he kissing you?"

"Yes, he was, and when you were in the elevator?"

"Yes…tongue down my throat, hmm, what should we do?" she asked.

"I'm not sure but if you want him you can have him."

"No, that's too easy, he needs to learn a lesson."

I could see the wheels turning as Juliet told me her ingenious plan. As per her instructions I approached "Slurpy" (his name was upgraded from Assgrabber due to the tongue kissing incidents) and lead him back to Juliet's bedroom. He was so excited to get naked but I told him to wait because I had a surprise for him. Juliet entered the room and sat next to me on the bed. Slurpy's eyes about bugged out of his head.

"You are a real stud aren't you," Juliet taunted.

"Umm, well…I think so," said the Slurp.

"Well stud guess what? You could have probably had Marie, or you could have had me, but you were a greedy bastard and thought you could have both. Now you get neither of us, and you better get your ass out of my place this instant." Her stern voice quite possibly retreated his manhood straight back into his pelvis.

Quickly Slurpy found his friend and the two of them left. Juliet and I laughed and looked to share the news with Blondie. We tapped on the bathroom door and asked if she was okay…mumble, mumble, something…something…fine, was all we heard. I logged onto our community sight and let some friends know what a good time we were having before passing out next to Blondie.

This is my favorite erotic photo of myself,
No makeup, no fancy clothes…

The Vulva. The external genitals of the female are called the vulva. The vulva consists of the labia major (meaning the larger lips), which are on the outside and which in the grown-up girl are covered with hair, and the labia minora (the smaller lips), which are on the inside and which are usually only seen when the labia majora are taken apart.

[Vulva in Lain means folding-door. The ancients were fond of giving fancy names to things.]

The Mons Veneris. The elevation above the vulva, which during puberty becomes covered with hair, is called by the fanciful name, mons Veneris, or Venus' mountain. It is usually padded with fatty tissue.

The Clitoris. The clitoris is a small body about an inch in length, situated beneath the mons Veneris and partly or entirely covered by the upper borders of the labia minora.

Woman: Her Sex and Love Life

Technically

We met the evening of Thanksgiving, I'd spent time with to little family and he'd spent time with possibly too much, either way we were happy to meet online and share our tryptophan induced after-dinner lethargy. Chris was twenty-four and a med student in Ohio. He had brown eyes and light brown hair and we were the same height. I liked that he asked me all kinds of questions about my life and I felt he genuinely cared about my answers. When I learned that he was studying oncology so he could be a cancer physician part of me thought possibly dad, mom and granny (who all died of cancer) had sent him to me.

We didn't chat long the time we met because he had plans to see a movie with friends, but he messaged me back as soon as he was back home. I don't remember how long we chatted but I liked him. He was open to the idea of an older woman, and I thought he was—cute and intelligent—two qualities that equal sexy. After a few online meetings we agreed to talk on the phone. His voice was not the deep lusty panty wetting voice of my dreams but I enjoyed him. We flirted and told each other how lonely we were. He asked if I would like to try phone sex with him and I explained that I'd tried it on a couple different occasions and enjoyed the playing but hadn't actually reached an orgasm. This put him on a mission, LOL.

I had never felt the need to masturbate to the point of orgasm. My husband, although a complete prick, did know how to push my buttons. I had never learned to. I had the toys in my nightstand and enough creams and gels for a large orgy yet I'd never used them by myself. I wasn't very comfortable about pleasing myself. I'd always been more worried about pleasing everyone else. This needed to change. Chris made it his goal.

I'd spent some erotic hours on the phone with other men since my divorce, but like my real life I found I worried more about giving them what they needed than I did about getting what I needed. I'd moan and ooh and ah over what they told me, and I'd tell them how excited they made me (which some did, just never to orgasm) and I'd have satisfaction in hearing them cum for me. More than once I faked my orgasm just so my phone partner felt good about himself. Chris was going to have none of those games.

He sweetly and slowly started to seduce me, he wanted me relaxed, he wanted me real. He suggested that I warm up my dildo with a hot towel before we got to carried away. It did feel better but try as he may he did not get me off. I was frustrated and so was he. He had all kinds of ideas on how I should be sitting or laying and at what angle I should insert my toy. I just became more frustrated and would beg him to cum for me and not worry that I hadn't. Reluctantly he eventually came and after he would swear next time it wouldn't be one sided. It didn't bother me when he came without me. I knew he was trying. I knew he cared. The problem was in my head, I had some mental block that I couldn't seem to get over.

One of my fondest memories of our phone time came when I was trying to impress and excite Christopher. I'd tell him how I was kissing him lightly on the lips…licking my way down his chest…down his stomach…across his hip bone…to his inner thigh…and then tickling my tongue on that sweet spot between his balls and ass—where he would interrupt and say, "You mean my (insert technical anatomically correct word here)." Um, yeah baby…that's sexy, LOL, I guess that's what you get when you mess with a professional.

We talked about meeting many times and once we got as close as him booking a very expensive last minute flight and being on the plane while I waited at my local airport. Unfortunately his plane became covered with ice and then returned to the hanger. It seemed a clear sign from God that we weren't meant to meet so we didn't push our lack of luck. He was busy with his mice and cancer research and I was busy figuring out who I wanted to be when I grew up. I dated, and when they ended he was still my friend and shoulder to lean on.

I remember being in tears one night chatting with him. I think we'd "known" each other at least two years and it had become obvious we weren't going to be more than chat friends. I had by that time broken my orgasm barrier (with someone else) and we'd had some fun times but I knew I would never be the wife of the famous doctor that cures cancer. Many tears have been shed over what could have been…many more than over what was.

We kept in touch for several years and I would still love to meet him. During one of our last online conversations I told him I hoped that someday I could have dinner with him and his wife (which I hope for his sake he has met by now) and they could show me pictures of their children. Funny how I say that and yet I can feel my eyes filling up. Or maybe one day he and his twin brother are both single…and I'm single…and…mmmmmmmmm…that's not just a male fantasy. ;-)

I do not want you to get the false idea that all men or most men are bad and mean, and are constantly on the lookout to ruin young girls. No, most men are good and honorable and too conscientious to ruin a young life. But thee are some men, young and old, who are devoid of any conscience, who are so egotistic that their personal pleasure is their only guide of conduct. They will pester you. Some will lyingly claim that they are in love with you; some perhaps will sincerely believe that they are in love with you, mistaking a temporary passion for the sacred feeling of love. Some will even promise to marry you—some making the promise in sincerity, others with the deliberate intent to deceive. Still others will try to convince you that chastity is an old superstition, and that there is nothing wrong in sexual relations. In short, all ways and means will be employed by those men to induce you to enter into sexual relations with them.

Don't you do it!

Woman: Her Sex and Love Life

Rhode Island Rendezvous

I want you to experience this in the order I did, without any expectations so…here it is, my first encounter with Scott, aka Frosty, Dec 3rd.

Frosty whispers to Marie~~: hello
Marie~~ whispers to Frosty: hello!
Frosty: how are you?
Marie: I'm good.. how are you?
Frosty: I'm doin great thx :)
Marie: who are you????
Frosty: I'm me lol
Marie: okay…. but.. have i done you??? Lol
Frosty: ummmm i dont think so just starting up some conversation…are you ok with that?
Marie: lol.. yes….
Frosty: cool :)
Frosty: where ya from?

Marie: MN and you??
Marie: hang on.. brb
Frosty: Rhode Island
Frosty: ok
Marie: im back.. sorry it took so long
Frosty: its ok :] wb
Marie: party at my house i guesss…lol…silly kid
Frosty: how old?
Marie: she is 15
Frosty: cool my little girl is 7 and my son is 3
Marie: how old r u?
Frosty: im 30 and i feel a moof coming
Marie: oh no.. im 32.. and not coming…
Frosty: lol thats fair :]
Marie: lol…married?
Frosty: divorced
Marie: same here
Frosty: how ya dealing with it? if I'm intruding you don't have to answer
Marie: I've never been single.. it's strange
Frosty: this is the first time i lived on my own i don't mind it its just the loneliness that is hard some days
Marie: yes.. i hate that….. i was with my x.. 16 years
Frosty: 8 years here
Frosty: that's a long time for you
Marie: yes…it was
Frosty: dating yet?
Marie: just a little…and you?
Frosty: same here i have one next monday I'm so nervous lol
Marie: good luck
Frosty: ty :]
Marie: i just need a good lay…lol
Frosty: would you like my pic i don't know about you but i like a face of the person I'm talking to
Frosty: lol yea me too
Marie: sure…please send…. you want mine then?
Frosty: yes please
Marie: wowie…. hot pic…very ssexxxxyyy
Frosty: awwww shucks lol
Frosty: now you have a sexy pic :] wow

Marie:ty
Frosty: yw
Marie: hence.. the title…lol
Frosty: lol i didn't want to presume anything
Marie: lol….. i know.. im bad…sorry.. <eg>
Frosty: its all good
Marie: brb
Frosty: ok
Marie: ok.. I'm back
Frosty: wb
Marie: teenagers!!! omg…my kids friend.. was just dumped…she was in here cryin
Marie: and it was there 3 week anniversary too..!!! (lol)
Frosty: dont you wish you could go back? NOT hehe
Frosty: 3 weeks omg the tragedy of it all lol
Marie: this is bad enough….
Marie: lol.. i know.. and i thought it would last forever….
Frosty: suggest counceling hehe
Marie: LMAO
Frosty: lol
Marie: trauma squad…to the rescue
Frosty: is there hope for the young lovers?
Marie: nope…he had no feelings for her…..
Marie: omg…he's legal…maybe i could be.. rebound woman!!! woohoooo
Frosty: the bastard i knew he was going to do this to her you could just see it coming hehe
Frosty: lol
Marie: LMAO
Marie: you are great, very funnny…i luvs funny…
Frosty: send her to me I'll dry her eyes (something else may get wet hehe but her eyes will be dry hehe)
Marie: omg…. lol
Frosty: lol
Frosty: so how long has it been for you without sex?
Marie: 2 fuckless months…lol…
Frosty: woooo hooooooooooo :)
Frosty: one fuckless year!!! : (
Marie: 6 since a frickin orgasm….. I'm desperate…needy…. horny as hell….
Marie: OMG!!! and you haven't exploded…??!!!!

Frosty: orgasm man to the rescue! the first woman i end up with will explode hehehe

Marie: LOL>>>>> and the first man with me.. will drown....

Frosty: lmao

Frosty: what a way to go

Marie: damn...that wouldn't look good would it??.... woman dies from strange vaginal explosion.. while man found near her...cum in his lungs.... drown....

Frosty: lmao

Frosty: film at 11

Marie: well.. yeah.. of course we'd been filming...lol

Frosty: woman's head was decapitated

Marie: LOL...yet.... strangely...smiles were on both corpses....

Frosty: lol

Frosty: kids do not play with loaded guns

Marie: hmmmm sounds like a sundance flick...

Marie: LOL...i would love to play with a loaded gun

Marie: but...id just end up.. unloading it

Frosty: *Frosty is glad he whisperd you your cool :)*

Frosty: i have a semi automatic it reloads after being fired

Marie: ty sweetie...i think the same about you...and damn.. your so cute!!!

Marie: omg.... not a single shot??? cooooool

Frosty: awwwww shucks :) lol

Frosty: well i use to be able to go for hours lol key word being use

Marie: ohhhh.... sorry to hear that..... lol

Frosty: i need to test the unit again lol

Marie: ßhangs sign on door.. " unit testing"

Frosty: knock knock

Marie: cum in

Frosty: why ty hehe

Marie: lmao..... what seems to be the trouble sir?

Frosty: my drains clogged

Marie: ohhh my......have you tried suction?

Frosty: just alot of one hand techniques

Marie: ohh no no no...that wont help this problem...you've got it backed up...wayyyy beyond that

Frosty: that's what i thought any recommendations?

Marie: well...let me see...<down on knees>.......

Frosty: *Frosty looks down and smiles*

Marie: i think you need an oral exam
Frosty: am i covered for this procedure?
Marie: hmmmmmmm….. i cant see your policy from here…sorry
Frosty: hell with it I'll pay cash
Marie: okay then….. <back to work>
Frosty: you're the boss :)
Marie: mmmmm……….. i think…suction.. is definitely what you need…..
Frosty: will i need a local?
Marie: what…you don't want me anymore…??? lol
Frosty: lol
Frosty: you're the professional here
Marie: geeezzzz….. im still trying to help you….
Frosty: please continue
Marie: i think some stimulation.. along with the throat thrusting.. will give you some relief
Frosty: i think maybe your right
Marie: mmmmmm…deeper…baby….
Marie: maybe the moaning vibrations.. will help relieve the pressure
Frosty: yummmmmmmm yes please
Frosty: shall i try?
Marie: yesssss.. help me.. please…
Frosty: how can i help? maybe by licking your neck a little and running my hands up and down your thighs?
Marie: mmmmmmm……okay…. lets trade for your fee….
Frosty: let me lay you down while my tongue traces your lips my hands running through your hair..my leg rubbing on yours…then kissing you passionately
Marie: mmmmmmmmmmmmmm…well.. let me melt you tooo frosty…. woooohoooooo
Frosty: i kiss your neck feeling the wetness of my tongue on your neck while my hands trace your body over your clothes..slowly i remove your shirt i kiss down the center of your chest moving my lips back up to kiss you some more
Marie: hmmm didn't you say.. when we first started chattin.. you felt a moof coming???? or was that…muff???
Frosty: lol
Frosty: shall i stop? lol
Marie: oohhh god no….
Frosty: you sure?

Marie: uuummmmm…aahhh.. pppIleeeeeaasseee donnnntttttt
Frosty: my hands move to your breasts my tongue teasing yours…i move my mouth to your nipples…gently tracing the outside flicking my tongue on the tip entering the whole nipple in my mouth…i tease your nipples feeling them grow harder in my mouth my hands run down the length of your legs and grasp on your ankles…
Marie: omg…omg…I quiver with anticipation…
Frosty: moving my tongue down your stomach…i stop to unzip your pants slowly taking them off one leg at a time all the time ours eyes don't leave each others i raise myself up to kiss you and move my way down stopping to place gentle kisses on your stomach my hands running between your legs my fingers running through your hair…
Marie: ohhhhh i love your eyes…. and the reflections in them….
Marie: the hot desire….. entices me…..
Frosty: my kisses continue down your thighs kissing your calves my hands cant keep off of you…i make my way back up your legs my tongue leading the way…kissing ever so close to your precious lips i gently begin to rub your walls i place your legs on my shoulders as my tongue traces the rim of your walls…
Marie: mmmm…god yessss…my legs reach around you….. i pull you in closer…
Frosty: spreading your lips my tongue enters you slow soft licks i can feel the wetness of you mmmmm you taste sooo good i gently begin to rub your clit soft circular motions as my tongue is in and out of you i raise my hands up to caress your breasts
Marie: ohhhhh yessssssssssssssssssssssss
Frosty: im getting worked up here lol
Marie: ohhhh you are wonderful…..
Frosty: i am?
Marie: just like in real life…I'm used to doing all the work…. this is great
Frosty: i prefer to please than to be pleased (in real life that is)
Marie: me toooo.. but.. i could get used to this….
Frosty: to what?
Frosty: do you usually do all the typing? lol
Marie: yes…lol…my fingers are all cramped and deformed from cyber.. lmao
Frosty: oh my lolol

Marie: cyberfuckle syndrome.. its awful....
Frosty: lol
Marie: hehehe
Marie: i mean.. ive never cybered before.. please continue....
Frosty: lmao and im the pope lolol
Marie: nice to meet you your pontif....
Frosty: yw my child
Marie: <kisses ring> ring.. a ding ding.. that is...lol
Frosty: *Frosty slaps her forehead—be healed from your cyber ways*
Marie: ouch...LOL
Marie: i have a pic i think you'd like...wanna see it???
Frosty: should've took the ring off my bad lol
Frosty: sure...and this a pic of????????
Marie: well.. im naked......in it.....
Marie: and...you can seee my pussy.....
Frosty: you!!!!!???????? who took it?
Marie: still want it???
Frosty: uh huh lol
Frosty: you're a sexy one huh
Marie: i don't think so...do you?
Frosty: i do
<file nakedpussypic sent>
Marie: aaaawwww.. ty
Frosty: lmao I've been had!!!!!!!!!!!!!! I see your head and a CAT!
Marie: LMAO...i didnt lie!!!
Frosty: lol here kitty kitty lolol
Marie: you like...my pussy????.. i know.. its a little hairy...
Frosty: can i rub your pussy
Marie: ahhhh...gooooood
Frosty: and what talents do you have?
Marie: deeeeeeeeep throat.. like the keilbasa queen..
Frosty: yummmmmmm
Marie: hmmmm...i have many talents....which do you desire???
Frosty: ahhh yes my tongue was pleasing your pussy my fingers rubbing your clit...i run my hands under your ass and gently pull you up to bury my face in you....wanting to take you there...waiting for your legs begin to quiver
Marie: mmmmmm.... let me lick your finger off......teasing you... pleasing you...

Frosty: i raise my self up and put your breast in my mouth working your nipples while my fingers enter you...bending them so to be able to rub them against your clit as the pump in and out of you
Marie: ahhhhhhhhhhh...yesssss....... i shudder with excitement....
Marie: omg...i need the first orgasm...now....
Frosty: tracing my tongue back down your body wanting to taste more of you spreading your lips i enter my tongue wanting your juices wanting you to cum on my tongue
Marie: omg...yesssssss.....
Frosty: i place all my energy on your clit my fingers pumping in and out of you all the while i rub your clit i feel your body begin to shake yes baby cum babe ohhh yesssss
Marie: ohhhh yesssss...i grab the sheets.. i grab the pillow..... i scream...as i explode.. YYYEEEEEEESSSSSSSSSSSSs
Frosty: *Frosty smiles*
Marie: omg...yesssss..... ohhhhhhhhhhhhhhhhhhh
Marie: the room spins.. my mouth is dry.... lights flicker...omg.....
Frosty: cum babe cum
Marie: mmmmmmmmm.................... yesssssssss..... i release.. all....... and flood the bed with my excitement......
Marie: im sooo hot.....
Frosty: are you really?
Marie: i want to taste you toooo
Marie: you are wonderful...i am hot.....
Frosty: im here for the tasting babe
Marie: mmmm...let me lay you down then dear...
Frosty: i bet you say that to all the boys lol
Marie: uhhhh ALL...excuse me.... 200.. is not ALL...geeezzzz
Frosty: lol holy shit
Marie: just kiddin....im innocent
Frosty: lol so was o.j. lol
Marie: lol...let me rub this sticky stuff off.. and throw the rag in my blazer......
Frosty: lol
Marie: you know.. if my friend would drive for awhile.. i could use my laptop.. in the back seat.....
Marie: oohhhh yesssssssss yessss yesss
Frosty: ok im confused lol
Marie: ohhh sorry.. umm.. oj.. innocent.. rag.. friend.. blazer.. never-mind.. where was i...??

Frosty: i thought i was supposed to lay down?
Marie: yes…you were….
Marie: i kiss you deeply…passionatly…hotly…………..
Marie: then.. lightly…. pulling on your lower lip….
Marie: then moving to your neck…kissing and licking you….letting you feel the heat of my passionate breath on your neck
Frosty: mmmmmmmmmm
Marie: nibbling…your earlobe…whispering softly…i have to have you…i want you…
Frosty: *Frosty gets a chill*
Marie: moving.. slowly down your chest….. kissing wetly.. and licking you lightly….
Marie: running my finger tips.. along your arms……then on your chest….
Frosty: *Frosty runs his hands through your hair*
Marie: kissing your stomach…. nibbling at you…caressing you…moving dowwn…
   to your inner thighs…..nibbling and kissing them…
Frosty: that tickles hehehe
Marie: then.. moving.. back up…stroking your hot throbbing cock…watching your eyes.. as i move my lips closer to it…kissing all around the base of it…..teasing you…
Frosty: tracing your face with my fingers
Marie: then….. taking just the tip of my tongue…….. and running it lightly.. up and down its shaft….
Frosty: mmmmmmmmmmm nice
Marie: omg…the face thing…made me slide off my chair…. aaaahhh-hhhhh
Frosty:Marie: still stroking you..taking my tongue.. and swirling it around the head of your cock…..still watching you….taking you into my mouth.. just a little.. then back out…
Frosty: still tracing my fingers on your face watching your tongue
Marie: then…a little deeeper…..still playing with it with my tongue…then deeper….in and out…you can feel how hot and wet my mouth is….
Frosty: taking your hands in mine i raise my hips up to meet your lips
Marie: mmmmmmmmmmm…….i watch your face…then plunge your throbbing member all the way down my throat…until my lips touch it base….

Marie: you can feel my throat contract around it.. gripping you…

Frosty: my eyes close my head tilts back a deep moan comes out mmmmmmmmmmmmm

Marie: mmm…then back out again…..and in again…just as deeep….

Frosty: ohhhhh goddddddddd

Marie: i grab your ass and press you into my face……i cant get you any deeper into my throat….

Frosty: ohhhhh myyy godddddddddd

Marie: mmmmmmmmm……it makes me sooo hot to suck on you…my legs are wrapped around one of yours.. and i begin to rub myself up and down your leg while i suck you…

Frosty: immmmm so hard right now babe

Marie: mmmm…. im sooo happy…

Frosty: i need to take care of this

Marie: i take you out of my mouth…….. and move back up your stomach….licking and kissing you….. rubbing my pelvis against you

Marie: reaching your neck…. licking it….i whisper…ohhh god…i want to fuck you….

Frosty: mmmmmmmmmmmm

Marie: my legs straddle you…i reach down and take a hold of you….i take you in my hand…i rub you against my steaming clit….

Marie: slowly….. i let you enter me….ahhhhhhhhhhhhhh…. i moan with delight…yeeeessssss…i shiver…as it almost hurts…. as i take it all the way in…i grab your hands.. and help you rub my breasts.. as i begin to rock up and down.. back and forth on it….i throw my head back.. and bite my lip……..omg…yesssssss….

Frosty: mmmmmmmmmmmmmmmmm

Marie: fuck me….

Frosty: im close baby

Marie: i reach my hands behind my head.. i sit straight up on you….i lift my hair up off my back……ohhhhhhhhh yeessss….

Frosty: for real baby dont stop

Marie: omg.. im going to come on you…..i lean forward.. and my nipples brush across your chest…i lift up and downn.. faster and faster….ohhhhh come for my baby…i want to feel you cum for me….ohhhh i want to feel you pulsate into me……im sooo hot for you

Frosty: ooooooooo goddddddddddddddddddddddddddd mmmmmmmmmmmmmmmmmmm ahhhhhhhhhhhhhhhhhhhhh

Marie: allll of it baby….. all of it….mmmmmmmmmmmmmmmm

Frosty: mmmmmmmm arrrrrrrrrrrr ahhhhhhhhhhhhhhhhhhhhhhhhh
ooooooooooooooooohhhhhhhhhhhhhhhhh yyyyyyyeeaaaaaaaaaaaaaa
Marie: mmmmm................ feel better baby??
Frosty: oh god much ☺ ty ☺
Marie: good...ty
Frosty: yvw
Marie: ty for the whisper...lol...nice meeting.. you..... <k>
Frosty: do you have icq? nice meeting you :]
Marie: yes i do.... let me turn it on
Frosty: cool ·
Marie: like...you turned me on...
Frosty: can i add you? how about instant messanger? lol
Marie: you shoulda went there first...!! lol
Frosty: lol my bad...btw.. my name is scott..
Marie: mmmmm...you are fun.....hi scott.. . im marie
Marie: nice to do you!! lol
Frosty: lol same here
Marie: lol...so what kind of band do you play in?
Frosty: past tence
Marie: did?
Frosty: yup
Marie: *Marie~~ squeezes another word out of scott*
Frosty: i quit so i could be a better dad
Marie: wow...what a man...!!
Frosty: *Frosty blushes lol*
Frosty: lol gonna melt me?????/hehehe
Marie: wooohoooooo.. well i owe you...!!!!!
Frosty: you're in debt to me? this is good hehehe
Marie: lol..... what do you want for payment??
Frosty: your friendship :)
Marie: you are wonderful!
Frosty: naaaaaa
Marie: why did you whisper me.. in the first place
Frosty: i liked your profile
Marie: lol...wow.. and my world has been rocked...ty...llol...you are
very funny and intelligent..............
Frosty: really thats not what my ex says hehehehe
Marie: awww.. forget the bitch.... lol
Frosty: i cant she's the mother of my kids tell me god doesn't have
a sense of humor lol

Marie: lol.. dont go there…lol
Frosty: lol ummmmmmmm okey dokey
Marie: when is your bday?
Frosty: april 3rd why? gonna get me something hehehe
Marie: you put dec 25.. on your icq…. lol……jesus christ….
Frosty: yes my child hehehehe
Marie: lol
Frosty: i should change that huh
Marie: yes…how do you expect to get woman with this jesus complex???? lol
Frosty: lol i just changed it
Frosty: wanna see my kids? oh your not in room anymore i cant : (
Marie: i will come back.. invite me…
Frosty: ok
Marie: i bet they're adorable!
Frosty: of course they are thier my kids hehehe
Marie: lol.. they are soo cute…!
Frosty: ty :) thier my angels
Marie: do you spend much time with them??
Frosty: i get to see them 3 times a week :)
Marie: wow.. thats great!!!
Frosty: yes
Marie: amber's dad hasn't spent an hour with her since he left 6 months ago.. he will never be part of her life again.. and he is missing the best thing he ever had
Frosty: hes gonna regret it
Marie: yes he will…but he doesn't deserve her…she is fantastic..
Frosty: she deserves a dad though : (
Marie: maybe i will get lucky.. and find her a good one…
Frosty: don't you ever settle make sure he's great!!!!!!!!!!!!!!
Marie: ty hun………….
Frosty: yvw :)
Marie: so…you moving here..?? or me there??? lol
Frosty: hehehe you tell me lol
Marie: well.. my farm is paid for.. and I've got a horse for each kid.. how about you come here….
Frosty: i coudn't leave my munchkins its a nice thought ty
Marie: well.. duh.. i said bring them….
Marie: amber is most important thing in my life….
Frosty: thats great hun she needs love in her life

Marie: i spoil her rotten...
Frosty: nothing wrong with that as long as you keep her level headed which I'm sure you do.
Marie: yes i do.. she is an A student.... and sits third chair flute on the senior concert band...
Frosty: omg that is so great great job mom your ex is such a loser if he doesnt be part of her life
Marie: well.. he never really has been...too much work you know....
Girl Scouts, 4-H, FFA, band, riding lessons, piano lessons, swimming lessons...etc.. he was never there
Frosty: ok you get my vote super mom :)
Marie: ty dear.. i try
Frosty: well i can talk to you all night but i have work tomorrow i think i hear my pillow calling me
Marie: okay hun.. great meeting you!!!! if i was your pillow.. id be calling you tooo!!!!
Frosty: great meeting you too!!!!!!! ty for the company
Frosty: lol :)
Marie: no.. thank you dear :-)
Frosty: yw you gonna be on tomorrow?
Marie: i might be.. unless i get a life.. umm yeah.. i probably will be....
Frosty: lol well if you get one find one for me too please
Marie: ok dear...happy thoughts....
Frosty: nothing but :)
Frosty: sweetdreams
Marie: b~bye!!!
Frosty: night. bye Marie
Marie: bye scott!

I went to work the next day thinking about Rhode Island. That had been a long conversation even for me. I laughed...I played the cyber thing...and...we chatted more after that. Which is always a good sign. I logged on as soon as I finished chores at home and found an ecard from Scott. Cool!!! I opened the link and found a picture of a little basset puppy. Underneath it was written: Now tell me this isn't the cutest thing you've ever seen!—Scott. Aww...that was so sweet. I looked for him to chat with but he wasn't online. ☹

We did connect later and we had even more fun than the previous night. He was so funny and sweet and he kept telling me how cool and sexy I was...ahhh, what a guy! By the next night we exchanged phone numbers and I called him. The New Englander accent was cute. He had a great laugh and when he sang to me…that was it…I was hooked. We talked for hours and hours. I gave him my 800 number at work and the next day he called me there three times! Mmmm…I love when you know they are thinking about you.

That week we talked about sixty hours on the phone. Any minute I wasn't talking to him I was wishing I was. Everyday when I got home there would be a new ecard. Thinking of you, I like you a lot…etc…all very cute and sappy. The songs he sang me to sleep with were my favorites from high school. I felt wanted again. One night after a few hours of very deep conversation he said he had something to tell me…my heart skipped a beat, than about leapt from my chest. I knew it was coming and I could barely stand the wait…"I love you," he said softly. Tears welled in my eyes, I was quiet, than I said, "I love you too."

I couldn't believe that I let myself say it. Love was a four-letter word that carried all kinds of weight with it. After the crap with my ex it wasn't something I took lightly. I wasn't going to say it if I didn't mean it, I meant it. The ecard the next day read: For my love, I love you so much baby! Thank you for finding me—Scott.

We continued talking several times throughout the day and usually ended our nights laying in bed playing phone sex or having me listen to him sing to me. It was so romantic and sweet I wanted to do something special for him. I decided to fly to see him. I talked to my good buddy Blondie and decided for safety sake to meet her and than go with her to a casino to first meet Scott. I booked the flight and found a very nice hotel with a jacuzzi suite. Blondie booked a regular room and we figured if Scott wasn't who I thought…she and I would share the suite and he could have the other room.

Blondie picked me up at the airport and we spent a couple days in New York together. When I used to sit home and watch movies with my ex we'd talk about New York and wonder why anyone would want to go to such a crowded place, but…I loved it! All the people watching…all the hustling about…people of all shapes, colors and sizes…I was mesmerized. I was so proud of myself for just being there. I was taking a chance. I was out of my element, but I was happy.

We drove to the hotel near the casino where I was to meet Scott. I was so nervous. I was about to meet the man that had told me a few days earlier, "I want to spend the rest of my life with you." Blondie worried about me, but I assured her this was going to be great for me.

Waiting at the casino bar I went through several drinks. He got there a little late but I recognized him from his photos right away. He came and sat at our table. It was too odd that we had shared so much online and on the phone, yet now we sat like strangers. Blondie made fun of us and finally he touched my leg and gave me a kiss. Just like that the uneasiness was gone and we started talking like we'd been together forever. We gambled and drank the evening away. Back at the hotel we had a good time, however, it would have been better if we both hadn't drank as much as we did!

The next morning I met Blondie and told her that everything went well with Scott and she was free to go home…lol…her baby-sitting duty was over. I would go with Scott to his house and fly home from RI. We spent two wonderful days together, mostly just lying cuddled together on the couch watching movies, just enjoying being close. It was a tearful goodbye at the airport even though we had already decided I would fly back in two weeks so we could be together on New Years Eve.

The two weeks seemed much longer but we continued talking on the phone a few times a day. Our conversations were a little different now that we had been together. There weren't all the exciting unknowns like there had been. We already knew what it would be like to be together and we didn't have that to talk about. The conversations were shorter, but we still enjoyed each other. We spent a couple hours talking on Christmas day so we wouldn't be alone. That was a hard day, I was happy to know I wouldn't be alone on New Years.

My nerves were much calmer on the second flight to destiny. I wondered if he'd bring me flowers at the airport. I always enjoyed watching lovers meet after being apart. I was so happy this time I would finally have a reunion like that…right there, in front of all the other travelers. I got off the plane and looked around, no sign of Scott. I wandered to baggage claim and still no sign. I knew he ran late often and tried to keep a smile on my face. I was starting to wonder when the next plane to Minnesota would be leaving when he finally showed up.

He took one of my bags and gave me a little hug. I could have been his sister. I was very disheartened. Back at his apartment he still seemed more reserved than the last time I was there. I asked if anything was wrong and he brushed off his behavior as just being tired from work. We went to bed and the sex was just okay. I still hadn't learned to trust enough to orgasm and he didn't have the energy or will to work at it to hard. When we woke the next morning he asked if I'd like to go for a drive and see some sights. I loved doing that so we spent the entire day driving around areas that he grew up in. He wasn't cuddly while driving and I had hoped he would be, but he was showing me some of his past and places he was passionate about so that was almost as good as cuddling.

We were on his couch bringing in the New Year when his phone rang. I thought to myself, hmm…now who would call a single thirty-year-old man at midnight? He didn't answer the phone till we were finished, than he took it into the other room to listen to his message. He came back to me and told me it had been his brother just checking in on him. I tried to believe him but didn't. Now he sat in his chair and I on his couch. There was more distance between us than when we first met and he was in RI and I was in MN. I decided to bring it up.

"I know you're different with me now than the first time I came to see you, what has changed?" I asked.

"Nothing, I'm fine," he said.

"I'm not stupid, something is different and I'd appreciate you just being honest with me," I begged.

"What's wrong with you I said nothings wrong, I'm not different, nothing has changed," he stated coldly.

"Yeah right, I think you have someone else and that's who called. Please just tell me what's going on." I tried to hold back the tears. I could tell in the defensiveness of his voice that I had guessed correctly. "I know that's what it is, why do you deny it?"

"Fine, its true."

"Why did you lie to me? Why did you let me fly all the way back here again if you didn't want me anymore?"

"It was a good lie. I thought what the hell I'd have some sex this weekend too, no big deal, no ring on my finger," he smugly grinned.

I held back the tears and turned back toward the television set, determined to not start crying and giving him any more satisfaction. He went and got a bottle of rum and started mixing himself some strong drinks. After he left the kitchen I went in and did the same. I returned to the couch like I lived there. He seemed irritated that I wasn't yelling at him. He went into his office room and fired up his computer. I watched another movie and than went and sat by him. I figured he'd maybe give me some details on what had changed, but he was an ass. He chatted away on the comp laughing and thinking he was cute. I had changed from mixing drinks to straight coke. I decided it was safer than being drunk and sick that far from home. Scott was now drunk and even his typing skills were beginning to show it.

I sat quietly watching him flirt with other women. Watching him trying to pretend he was fine. It didn't take long before he went to the bathroom and than stumbled onto his bed. He was passed out. I was wide awake and decided I'd log on and chat with my friends. When I went to his computer I noticed he had been to drunk to shut down any of his programs. His messengers and chat windows were all left open. I had access to everything.

Immediately I started chatting in the 30s room where he had found me. I typed in the drunken slurred letters that he had, being sure to follow some of his standard chat-english. Everyone assumed it was still Scott typing so I began to have "Scott" tell the room what an asshole he was. I figured that may be my best bet on having people figure him out. I'd be him drunk…so drunk he had decided to confess his sins to all of chat world. It was working. I got plenty of responses, and than some Diane began asking intimate questions. I told her I had lied to a friend in Minnesota, telling her that I loved her and that she was now here in my house watching movies in the other room. Diane became incredibly agitated and I knew she had been talking "serious" with him too.

Every hour or so Scott would stumble back into the bathroom, puke, pee, brush his teeth and head back to his bed. After every trip of his I made one of my own, I'd pee, run his toothbrush around the toilet rim, put it back in its holder and return to the computer. It was a childish and immature act yet each a small victory for me, and very fulfilling. Nice to be able to laugh when you really want to scream or cry.

I learned a lot about Diane. Even though it was apparent she was stoned and not real bright, it was also obvious that she had been spending a lot of what had been "my time" on the phone with Scott over the days since my last visit. After I explained I was the woman from Minnesota and not drunken Scott we bonded together and planned ways to pay the bastard back for messing with us.

The next day online I met Jean. She messaged Scott, only it wasn't Scott it was I and this is our conversation:

Jean says: how are you?
Scott says: terrible and you?
Jean says: terrible??
Scott says: id I ever tell you about marie from minnesota?
Jean says: no, why? Did I ever tell you I have a fractured wrist and 2 fingers?
Scott says: what happened?
Jean says: Matt
Scott says: sorry to hear that hun…this isnt scott…it's the stupid chick from minnesota that believed scott when he said he loved her and flew out here for the second time to see him…etc…used…hurt.. and crying now
Jean says: excuse me? Who are you?
Scott says: surprise to you? Was he planning to meet you too?? Or has he??
Jean says: not really, what's your name
Scott says: marie
Jean says: where is he? Isn't he off today?

Scott says: sure he is...after I found out he was playin me with someone named Diane.. he started drinking heavy...than puking.. etc.. maybe somewhere in that stone heart he did feel bad. He thought he could fuck me one weekend and her the next.. damn .. I thought I was special

Jean says: me too—asked me to marry him once—oh well, he's got problems, I like him as a friend though—I don't know what I'd do without him, but you saved me a trip to RI next month.

Scott says: damn hun.. you toooo.. fuck.. there are lots of us

Jean says: I'm having a real hard time moving on, but I guess he's having fun

Scott says: when did he ask you to meet him there? Ive been serious with him since dec 3.

Jean says: he dumped me dec 6, but I was still going to come out there though

Scott says: my life sucks to hun.. just got my divorce final after 14 yrs of marriage.. hmm.. I think he talked about you.. I know he told some of his lady friends that he had met someone.

Jean says: how many others are there that you know about?

Scott says: I don't know.. im researching it now.. lol, but hes been phone sexin diane.. the same nights hes had me.. and singing her the same love songs.. etc.. that's what fucking hurts

Jean says: I know, do you have any idea what he's done with my ring?? I want it back.. I thought he was seeing gina??? where is he today?

Scott says: hes still asleep.. what does the ring look like?.. dayamm.. gina?.. I don't know that one.

Jean says: it has 5 round diamonds in a row—gina lives there somewhere—he dumped me for her, he was supposed to send it back but never did

Scott says: how did he get the ring?

Jean says: I mailed it to him...I was gonna move there, now I live in CO with my 3 kids.

Scott says: to be with him?

Jean says: yup

Scott says: when was this hun?

Jean says: oct-dec

Scott says: he told me he had no idea you were serious...hmmm

Jean says: and he asked me to marry him......hmmm.. I have it all in writing, what is going on with him??????? Is he depressed????

Scott says: I'm just finding out...he latched on to me really tight.. we talked on the phone 10 hours a day.. etc.. even at work 3-4 times a day.. I thought he was wonderful

Jean says: me too.. I think he is a good person just has problems, I do love him, but I'm glad I found out about him.. I spent 100's of $ on phone cards to talk to him.. go wake him up and say.. jean wants to know where her ring is.. she's here!! See how fast he jumps.

Scott says: oh fuck hun.. lol.. maybe later.. hell he probably hocked it.. he has no fucking money.. I will look for it...womans ring?

Jean says: yea, he said he had it in an envelope with my pictures to send back. I thought he made good money? Where does he really work? Did you have to pay to fly there or did he?

Scott says: hell no.. I paid for everything.. including the jacuzzi suite at the hilton the first night we met.. and I spent about $400 on his kids for xmas...and bought him tickets to my house for his vacation. He has no money.. he is filing bankruptcy soon

Jean says: I knew about the bank thing, he was seeing gina at xmas.. the week before, he went to a casino or something with her for the weekend.

Scott says: no hun.. that was me

Jean says: he told me you were gina

Scott says: hmm.. why would he call me gina?.. strange

Jean says: how did you access his messenger?

Scott says: I logged on and it just came up.. guess I was supposed to find out.. fate?

Jean says: has to be.. lol what did he tell you about me?

Scott says: are you still married?

Jean says: yeah.. splitting up.. I got a house.. he's the one who fucked up my arm

Scott says: how old are you? I'm 32

Jean says: he said you were 23.. no kids.. id love to hear what he's told you about me!

Scott says: wish I could remember more.. one night he went through his women lists and told me something about everyone of them.. I think he just said you had been through hell with an abusive husband and were a good friend

Jean says: he didn't tell you I was psycho? I was still coming there even though I knew he was seeing someone else.. dumb, huh?

Scott says: he still said you could huh??? Why don't we women ever listen to our guts and notice those goddamn huge red flags!!???

Jean says: I know!! how long have you been in RI with him? I was just gonna come as a friend.

Scott says: I was here the 4 day weekend before xmas and I've been here since Friday night.. we were fucking on the couch at midnight, when his other woman called to wish him a happy new year

Jean says: which other one??

Scott says: diane from vermont.. I spent all night on the phone with her.. she's hurting now too.. he was trying to see her in between seeing me

Jean says: wow!! busy boy! in sept.. it had been a whole year since he had slept with anyone

Scott says: I got that story too.. he told me he didn't cheat on his wife either.. but diane said he'd admitted to here twice he did at xmas parties for work

Jean says: WOWWW whole different scott opening up here. What are you gonna do or say?

Scott says: I haven't decided yet.. any suggestions?

Jean says: just PLEASE let him know that you talked to me—it will surprise him! Let him know what I said about my ring, when are you supposed to be leaving?

Scott says: 5pm today, okay I will tell him

Jean says: give it to him gooood

Scott says: I was thinkin of letting him have the tickets to minnesota.. than just not picking him up.. lol..

Jean says: can I ask you something personal? I know this is lame but.. is he "good"?? just asking because he was always bragging.

Scott says: well he tried.. but kept going soft.. and has no fucking stamina.. lol.. I was disappointed.. and its thin.. and has a weird bend to it.. no where near the 8 he said

Jean says: really??? surprising.. he said I would need insurance and medical attention!!!

Scott says: sure.. for splinter removal!! hahahhaahaha

Jean says: what did he promise you? The world??

Scott says: oh yeah.. he was going to rock it.. not just bump it a little.. LMFAO!!

Jean says: lmao too.. glad I found this out though I appreciate you talking to me, do you have a computer at home? We need to start a.. scotts ex's websight!

Scott says: yeah.. im gonna email you hun.. lol.. if you don't mind.. you and everyone else on all his fucking lists!! Hehehehe

Jean says: alrighty!! You go girl!! Email me and let me know what happens later. I'll be here until 5pm RI time.. or you can email me from home.. id love to know, this is soooo weird, what else have you found out???

Scott says: im still diggin.. skeletons fucking everywhere.. lol, did he do the damn singing on the phone thing with you too?

Jean says: yes.. irritating.. but made me laugh! He gave me a lot of good laughs when I needed them I have to give him that much!

Scott says: what a fucking weinie.. im such a stupid sap...I know.. me too.. I thought how special

Jean says: no you're not. I almost committed suicide

Scott says: I was right there too in June because of my ex, I was feeling so great.. now he's got me crashing over his worthless ass

Jean says: same here—I just put all our "stuff" away last weekend, I almost did it over HIM!

Scott says: sweetie.. he's def not worth it.. but he's under my skin too.. hell. He was in my skin.. hopefully I wont catch anything!!!

Jean says: do you have any kids?

Scott says: my 15 yr old daughter takes care of me.. she is gonna be so fuckin pissed that I let him hurt me

Jean says: ouch, I haven't loved someone in 7 years.. he got to me!

Scott says: me too.. what were we thinking??

Jean says: obviously we weren't.. did you meet him online?

Scott says: yup.. I thought he was great.. he found me on the 3rd.. we talked the 5th.. and been serious since

Jean says: how many tattoos does he have? Same happened here-started talking at the end of sept and he dumped me on dec 6

Scott says: 5 cheap ones

Jean says: oooh.. well at least he was honest about something! I want to know where my stuff is.. he should have mailed it back by now-he said he saved all our conversations and stuff and won't get rid of them.. what a joke!

Scott says: shit.. he lives.. I might have to disappear soon.. k?

Jean says: let me know! Stay strong!

Scott says: I will try...I peed on his toothbrush.. LOL

Jean says: LOL.. hahahhahaha good for you

Scott says: it did make me smile.. and when I heard him using it.. I was cracking up.. lol

Jean says: good for you.. keep in touch.. k

Scott says: I will.. heres my email () incase he gets my addy book or something

Jean says: ok.. thanks

Scott says: he had actually told diane after she said how long it had been since she had sex.. oh...so you're fresh than!!!, she thought that was odd but let it go

Jean says: sick boy!! avoid him like the plague!! Get out while you can!

Scott says: maybe his toilet toothbrush.. will give him the plague.. lol

Jean says: hahaha! Could we get so lucky??? Let him know you're talking to me

Scott says: okay.. it was tooo funny last nigth.. after I met diane here.. I called her from here.. we got all the details straight..than I gave him a chance to be honest with me.. asked what was up?? Did he still love me.. etc...he denied all.. than I sat in front of him.. hit redial.. and said.. hi...he still is denying talking to you.. haha-haha.. he almost shit.. but tried to play it real cool.. whatta guy

Jean says: he needs a RUDE awakening

Scott says: I know.. he cant just keep doing this to all us vulnera-ble women online, most of us are here because we've been hurt so bad.. now we are prey

Jean says: true.. very true. Where is he now?? What does his apt look like?

Scott says: very small and simple.. he doesn't even have beds for his kids, he's still in bed

Jean says: he told me that he always sleeps on the couch, does he? His kids never spend the night.. or so I thought

Scott says: he sleeps on the couch.. because his bed is sooo lonely.. wanted someone special to be in it with him the first time...I thought that was me.. but he told diane the same thing after I had already been in it.. so .. now I don't believe him.. I could be.. miss 100 or something. His kids only spend about 5 hours at a time here at the most

Jean says: ohhh I wonder who divorced who in that situation

Scott says: I'm starting to wonder too.. diane and I both wonder.. I was considering lookin for his x's phone number.. he first name is Lyn

Jean says: yeah.. I knew that much, see if you can find something about her

Scott says: I will...damn.. I met his kids yesterday.. they wanted to call me mom.. and he was in here on the comp smokin.. and I was playing with them

Jean says: he doesn't bother with them too much.. his daughter called me her stepmom!
You know.. I was even using his last name for mine

Scott says: OMG you are now!!?? I've been writing it.. thinking about it...SHIT!!

Jean says: not anymore!!

Scott says: geeee.. but he didn't realize how serious you were.. whoda guessed it?

Jean says: YEAH-HE ASKED ME TO MARRY HIM!! I have it in writing.. and he didn't know.. ggggrrrrrrr

Scott says: what a dink.. he played me with that too.. damn.. he didn't have to say that to get me to fuck him.. I would have done it for fun.. with all his big promises.. and now.. he just looks like a jerk

Jean says: yeah.. a BIG jerk

Scott says: well.. not that big .. hehehehe

Jean says: how funny!

Scott says: and he's not 5'10 either.. cause I am.. and he's shorter than me

Jean says: REALLY!!? How much shorter??

Scott says: I was disappointed.. but I'm an amazon.. lol.. an inch maybe.. hmm.. you want me to delete any pics you might have sent him??

Jean says: I only sent him one, a bad one, yeah delete it PLEASE

Scott says: what's the title? Are you the blonde one with the nipples?? lol

Jean says: no, I was with my friend, it's under surprise

Scott says: hmm.. I've looked at all of them.. only jean pic has a kid in front of her and she looks foreign

Jean says: geezz how many are there? is he very good looking in person?

Scott says: he looks about 22.. thought he was cute until the sight of him now makes me nauseous

Jean says: why??

Scott says: I'm just sick about what he's done to me and who knows how many others. What are you doing in the pic? I will find it.. how old r u?

Jean says: im 28.. just sitting in a chair at school, my friend is in it too, he probably deleted it

Scott says: are you dressed??

Jean says: YES!

Scott says: wheww...well.. there's lots of naked ones.. lol.. I've seen enough tits for one weekend.. lol

Jean says: you're kidding me!! Is he kinky or anything?

Scott says: oh yeah.. beats off all the time.. was ready to try any toy...that was what was fun.. I've taught him way to much...

Jean says: big mistake!

Scott says: he cant go a day without getting himself off at least once.. he cybers or phone sexes all the fucking time

Jean says: he told me he was a gentleman

Scott says: I was going to cuff him to a chair.. (I have my cuffs along.. lol) strip him naked.. and leave him in his apt hallway.. than call a cab.. lol

Scott says: he played gentleman with you??? Wowwww.. you're the only one giving me that story.. no phone sex???

Jean says: nope.. no phone sex.. delete all his pictures!!

Scott says: whatta prick.. I was collecting dick pics yesterday.. I was going to change the names on the dick pics to match chick pics.. than delete the chicks.. lol

*diane has been added to your conversation.

Scott says: hey diane.. scott asked jean to marry him too!! Jean.. this is diane.. she is scotts latest phone victim

Diane says: no shit.. omg.. good morning ladies?? How are you this fine eventful morning?

Scott says: lol...we are learning a lot

Jean says: ha ha!! hello!! we need to let him kow this is going on and shock him!

Diane says: where is he now?

Jean says: in bed

Diane says: hmmm.. shall I call and ask for him?

Scott says: no.. don't bother yet.. he hasn't said a word.. just gets up once in awhile.. pukes.. and uses the toothbrush I keep sticking in the toilet.. lol

Diane says: hehe no wonder why he is puking.. lol

Scott says: ahhh.. women unite

Diane says: how old are you jean?

Jean says: 28.. and you? Do you have kids?

Diane says: 35, yes

Scott says: he talked to her kids too jean.. we both got the.. I love the way you love your kids bullshit

Jean says: I told my kids about moving to RI

Diane says: ohhh man

Scott says: diane.. jean was already using his last name!!

Diane says: what the fuck? When was the fucking wedding planned?

Jean says: valentines day next year

Diane says: hmmm.. my anniversary truly is Valentines day.. my ex was very romantic.. lol

Jean says: ha ha ha.. did he promise you marriage?

Diane says: he didn't promise anything yet.. but I'm sure he was working some angle with me.

Jean says: how long has this been going on?

Diane says: talking.. close to 1.5 months.. sexually? About 2 weeks.. maybe a lil more or less.

Jean says: where do you live?

Diane says: vermont.. about 5 hour drive

Scott says: his dog is barking.. maybe he will get up..

Jean says: should have met marie there last night and really let him have it

Diane says: be careful there marie.. you don't know how pissed he's going to be

Scott says: pissed him??? why he hasn't done anything wrong.. remember?

Diane says: lol

Scott says: no ring on his finger

Jean says: never does anything wrong.. told me marie was gina

Diane says: yep.. just a ring on his dick.. to keep it hard.. lmfao

Scott says: no...we tried that.. it didn't help.. lol

Diane says: oh my fucking god.. no helping the poor son of a bitch now.. lol

Scott says: when he takes out the dog I will look for your ring
Diane says: what ring?
Jean says: he has my ring.. I sent it to him to save as collateral ..
ok.. thanks
Diane says: ten to one he pawned it.. wouldn't be surprised
Jean says: he said he still had it
Diane says: this guy thinks he is smoooooth
Scott says: he had all three of us scheduled at the same time
Diane says: where is it you found out about jean?
Scott says: she whispered me.. err.. him.. here last night. I've
written down all his women's names and emails.. I'm sending out
a.. to whom it may concern letter.
Jean says: hahahaha.. good one
Diane says: and me .. please I would love to know what is said
Scott says: I'm saving convos.. hmm.. I even have the first one
with him saved
Jean says: he saves mine too.. see if you can find and delete for
me.. please
Diane says: he still isn't moving?? Hmm.. do you think he remem-
bers anything?
Scott says: he just walked in here.. all mr happy.. I didn't close
down the screen.. lol
Jean says: good! let him know
Scott says: I will eventually.. he must pay.. he will pay..
Diane says: what a fuckin guy...unbelievable
Jean says: I want my ring back!!! Ggrrrrr
Scott says: after I go...one of you whisper him.. and invite the
other.. because that would shock the shit out of him.. you have
each other on your lists now right?.. he's back.. I have to go
soon.. but I'll stay long as I can
Jean says: tell him someone named jean is beeping him.
Diane says: ok.. here.. I may have to leave for a min or two.. but I
am here..
Scott says: I had a nice long talk with his friend.. elaine.. this
morning too
Diane says: no shit.. how many so far marie?
Scott says: she was just a friend.. but she thought he was a great
guy too.. errr.. used too.. lol
Jean says: yup.. gotta get the word out!! Quick!.. what is he
doing?

Diane says: it is out.. I spread it in 30s this morning
Jean says: good deal
Scott says: what did you say?
Diane says: good coverage.. worldwide.. oh my god is he gonna be sooo fucking shocked.. all because I said welcome home...lmfao..
Jean says: ha ha! You go girl!
Scott says: wait till my email goes out.. lol
Diane says: I asked if anyone knew frosty.. or scott.. and I said he is a major player .. and he is about to learn a valuable lesson from all involved.. and I mean all involved.. lol.. they said.. you go girl!
Jean says: he doesn't mind you on his computer, marie?
Scott says: hell no.. im not hounding him.. lol
Diane says: the stupid dumb fuck
Scott says: yup
Jean says: what is he doing???
Scott says: hes in watching tv now.. I have to shower yet.. damn I look like hell.. lol
Jean says: hasn't talked to you?
Scott says: not a word
Diane says: strange isnt it?
Scott says: yes he is
Jean says: lol
Scott says: I just need a ride to the airport.. lol
Jean says: definitely weird! gee.. Jean Marca.. what a joke!!
Scott says: hey.. marie marca aint happening either
Diane says: okay.. I admit.. I did write it out too...diane marca.. LMFAO!!
Scott says: suckers.. arent we
Diane says: no.. we're just looking for something we arent going to find here friends
Scott says: fuck.. why don't we have 3 men in chat talking about each of us instead..lol
Jean says: I have to go in a min.. but I'll be back in about an hour
Scott says: I'm going to go shower.. if you get on.. say hi scott first.. I will let you know is its me.. he might pretend to me me if he has any damn brains
Diane says: will he come on?
Jean says: don't worry.. he wont pretend
Scott says: he will probably look for you diane.. I will log everything off

Scott says: he pretended last night with diane while I sat here watching
Diane says: I'll stay for a short time girls.. ok.. trust in me girls
Scott says: he tried to keep her waiting for him
Diane says: bye jean.. sorry to have met you this way...
Jean says: it good now.. keep in touch!
Diane says: bye marie.. just be safe.. get home.. I don't want to read about you, ok
Scott says: I know.. that's all I worry about too
Jean has left the conversation
Scott says: I'm going to shower.. just give him sometime to dig himself deeper if you can stand it.. ok?
Diane says: no prob...talk to you later bye
Scott says: later!! thanks!

I packed my things and asked Scott if he'd give me a ride to the airport. He said he would. He kept looking at me funny. I took my bag and went to his car. The drive was quiet. I sat looking out my side window, wondering how I ever ended up in such a mess. Whenever I turned forward or toward him I kept on a happy face. There was no way I was going to give him any satisfaction. Once safely at the airport with my bags I said, "You think you're quite the player don't you."

He laughed, "Yeah, maybe I am."

I just laughed back and said, "We'll see who's playing who, goodbye."

He stood with a puzzled look and then got in his car and drove away. I sat next to a young man on the plane ride home. He just happened to be a hacker with some connections to some nasty computer viruses. I told him my sad tale and he offered his services any time I needed them. Just the thought of crashing Scott's world made me feel a lot better.

That night I composed my poison keyboard letter and sent it to every address I had collected from Scott's computer. While at Scott's I had emailed any pertinent information to my own personal account, including my conversations with Jean and Diane. The following was my attempt to even out the score with Scott:

Subject: Scott Marca

Good Morning Fellow Chat Addicts...lol
This is just a little informative letter about a certain acquaintance of ours...Scott Marca, RI.. aka.. Frosty. I met Scott a month ago in chat and spent about 60 hours that first week with him on the phone.. within a week.. he gave me a very heartfelt.. pull at my strings.. make me cry.. "baby, I love you".. like most of us here in chat I have been through hell with an ex.. and had been looking for someone sweet, kind, funny, intelligent.. WOW...he found me!!...yeah.. right.. NOT!!!
He would sing me love songs, cyber me, phone sex me.. he also had the nerve to tell me.. " I want to spend the rest of my life with you", " don't be surprised if I ask you to marry me", "I never thought id find you.. you're the one baby.. you're the one."
I'm very sorry if this hurts any of you but we woman need to stick together. I've been played before.. ya.. duh huh.. I let it happen again.. Scott just kept saying.. trust me.. and I did. I spent a four day weekend before xmas with him.. I flew there and spent a bunch of money on him (he has none—but that didn't matter to me.. all I seek is love) we had a great weekend.. very loving and sweet.. I ate it up!!! So much so that I went back to his place last weekend.. and bought him tickets to my place for his vacation next week. We happened to be screwing on the couch at new years when his phone rang.. he didn't answer it.. found out on Sunday that it hadn't been his brother like he said.. but another woman he had been phoning all week and planning on meeting soon. I talked with her, she was getting played too.. I got on his computer on Sunday and Monday while he was passed out or sleeping.. and met another woman that he had also said he loved and had talked of marriage.. these other ladies hadn't yet had anything physical.. but both were planning to within a couple of weeks.
I let Scott have a chance to come clean with me on what he had been up too.. he very coldly told me...nothing was wrong.. etc. Then after I let him know I knew.. he said.. "So, it was a good lie, there is no ring on my finger." WOWWW...this sweetheart hell of a guy is really a cold-hearted bastard. I couldn't believe it. The other women couldn't believe it either. The three of us women did a group conference chat and compared notes.. damn.. same shit all around almost, I'm not giving anymore details on their stories,

I'm just happy I met them before I got in any deeper, and I saved them the additional heart ache of a physical relationship.

Maybe to you Scott is just a friend, or just a cyber buddy or a phone sex friend...he does this a lot and that's fine.. as long as you don't bring the love and commitment crap into it like he did with me and at least one other woman.

This is just to let you know what kind of guy he really is and let you make a more informed decision about him.

He's great at the phone thing.. if that's all you want.. hell.. give him a call.. just remember.. no matter how much sugar he pours on his crap.. underneath it.. its still just CRAP!!!

If you have any other questions please feel free to email me.. and if you have any other great Scott stories please share with me.

Ohh, if you're wondering how I got all your email addresses.. I took them directly off his msn, icq, yahoo.. etc.. he has them all.. and no mens names.. just women...so please.. protect your hearts.. and good luck in your futures.

Love to all my sisters...lol...Marie

It didn't take long to get responses back.... Ohh...and a threatening phone call from Scott saying he knew people that could take care of me. Responses:

Subject: Scott.. the jerk

Hello
I got a hold of the email you sent out on Scott and this confirms that this guy is a real jerk. He really hurt my friend also, she lives in Canada and was reeled in by him also. Seems like he thinks he is all that and a bag of chips. He did some really cruel things to her. She spent a weekend with him also and was told he wanted to marry her and all the bull you were told and that he loved her and all that. Well the next week in chat he told everyone she was fat and ugly and a bunch more junk like that. I was in chat when it happened and he knows how I feel about her so when she kicked him out of chat he whispered me that I was not a friend to him and I said why not and he said well you are on her side and he called me every name in the book and told me I was stupid and all the bad language. My friend is now very happy and lives in another country because of her work and is getting married. Now when I

go into chat and he is there he makes fun of me and junk like that. Who needs him is what I said to him in the room and kicked him out about 10 times.. and he came back and said I love you and was poking fun at me. He is a real winner if you know what I mean. I am sorry you were one of his victims. But you are the bigger person letting everyone know the true Scott and for that I say thanks. Yes he needs to be stopped and he needs to be burned as he has burned others but the old saying what goes around comes around will happen sooner or later and he will get his. You have a nice day and thanks again for caring enough to let us all know the situation. You did the right thing. You will always be a better person for it. I don't have any problems in chat except him so that tell me it is not me. Don't beat yourself up about this ok, you did the right thing.. see ya.. S.

Subject: Re: Scott

About Scott...
...and this surprises you?? He did the same thing to a friend of mine-E—in chat a few months ago. I had a bad feeling about him from the start, but nobody would listen to me. "Not Scott, he's so nice." Is what everyone would say. He used to come into Womenonline on chat, that's where the son-of-a-bitch targeted his charm on my friend. But after he met her and got what he wanted, he dumped her like a brick!
Anyway, I found his address and phone number online. Let's all drive to his house and beat the shit out of him! Ohh, and be sure to tell him what a sick perverted bastard he is.
Tim

Subject: Re: Scott

I'm sorry to here Scott played you for a fool. I have heard this before about him. I don't go into chat much anymore, but, keep you chin up hun. There is someone special out there for you. Love to you, Lisa

Subject: Re: Scott

Marie,
   We are really sorry to hear about what happened with you and
Scott. My husband and I met "Frosty", in what used to be one of
our favorite chat rooms. He has always treated me with respect,
but maybe that is because he and my husband, had become good
friends.
   I know there are a lot of guys out there taking advantage of the
fact that on the net, you are really anonymous and that leaves a
wide open field. It is that you at least talk the steps you felt were
needed to protect others who might fall into the same type of
trap.
   As the female part of my marriage, I would like to say that I
admire the fact that you did speak out and try and warn others.
As for my husband, well he is a skeptic in everything and everyone. Maybe that is why he and Scott have seemed to get along
together. I am truly sorry that you and these others were hurt. It
makes me count my blessings all the more for the wonderful husband I do have here.
   I hope that God will send you that special person, and that you
find the happiness we all seek for our lives. Mrs P.

Subject: Re: Scott

Hi Marie,
I guess we all were played huh!? I got the same story, I love you
and want to meet you. We also talked for hours on the phone
(phone sex) and cybered. I let myself get involved with him cause
of a bad relationship also. I really did love him. When he didn't
come on for a while I thought something was up. This is the second time he did this but always had a good excuse. Was the story
about having two kids a lie also? I've been hurt too many times on
this damn puter I'm not allowing this to happen anymore, my trust
has been broken for the last time. These men think they can play
on our emotions like this, well maybe its time we give them back
what they give us. Don't get me wrong I'm not vindictive but now
its kinda revenge. I've had it. Thank-you for informing me about
this I really appreciate it. This really hurt to hear but I guess its

better to know now than go any further with it. Feel free to email me anytime. Again Thanks, D

I decided to write her back.

Subject: Re: Scott

Bless you for answering me.. he thought I would just run away and cry after he hurt me.. well no way asshole!
I figured there had to be others out there. I really fell for his line...he is good at it. After he heard about this email he went nuts!!! Called me at work and told me what a fat, repulsive cow I was and how he knew people that could take care of me.. guess I got to him. I can't believe how someone I opened my soul up to could be so cruel...we all need to let the world in on these player's games. Than they won't have so much fun playing all of us!! Oh, btw.. I met the two kids on Sunday, and they wanted to call me mom!! He doesn't even have bed for these kids. They never say over, and he never has any food or milk in the fridge.
Take care, Marie

Subject: Re: Scott

Marie,
I would very much like to talk to you about our "dear sweet Scott" I first met him in March/April. I think the things I have to tell you would interest you very much! LOL.. oh the stories I have. Let me know where you usually chat and when you are on and I'll find you. I'm so sorry he hurt you like he did...but I think I know where it all began. Talk to you soon hopefully...T

We connected online in chat about a week later. This is some of our conversation:

Tanone: we would talk about his wife and kids, and my kids.. but not my hubby because that made him jealous.
Marie: I know.. the first couple weeks I wasn't even supposed to talk to other men online
Tanone: back than, my hubby and I were going through a rough spot. His wife left him right after we started talking.

Marie: he tried to say that he left, and he wanted the divorce.

Tanone: she left and emptied the bank account-according to him. She took everything in the house even the phones one day while he was at work because she got on the pc and found emails from women.

Marie: wow.. you'd think he would have learned so I couldn't have done the same thing!

Tanone: you would think! lol

Tanone: I wasn't falling in love with him or anything, but I felt a bond with him and when I tried to explain it to him, it seemed to scare him off. A few months later he calls me out of the blue and wants me to phone sex him!

Marie: dang.. he must have broken up with someone earlier that day!

Tanone: that's what I was thinking.. so I told him to call back at 10 and then I didn't answer the phone, but that's when I knew he had changed a lot.

Marie: from what I've found out.. he gets connected with a woman.. grabs on tight.. keeps her all to himself for a week or two.. then.. finds someone else.. does the same with her.. but, never completely breaks it off with any of the previous ones, because he wants them still available if the current one doesn't work out.

Tanone: when I got your email I asked him what was up and how he could do that after what sas did to him and I was totally confused and he gets all defensive and says thanks for asking for his side of it and that he knows who his real friends are...sounds like someone else I used to know, men get the hang of the online playing thing really fast it seems

Marie: yeah they do

Tanone: I felt so bad when I got your letter because I knew it all started with me.

Marie: I didn't lie about anything in the letter he even called and threatened me

Tanone: I know it was true from the way he reacted he has a very violent streak

Marie: he threatened to burn my house down and cut off my horses' heads

Tanone: I don't know if he showed you that side before this happened

Tanone: OH Jesus!

Marie: no.. he was always an angel

Tanone: part of the reason his wife left was because he was violent

Marie: how did you find that out???

Tanone: she had a PPO put on him because she feared for her safety, he told me, but he said it was all bullshit and she was lying

Marie: wowwww...he leaves that part out of his new stories, I almost looked for her so I could call her. So...because of the violence is that why he doesn't have his kids overnight?

Tanone: I would suspect but I didn't realize they never spent the night.

Marie: Do you ever think he would carry out his threats?

Tanone: the Scott I knew I wouldn't think so, now I'm not sure, but I still don't think he would do it, he would be too afraid of losing his kids for good.

Marie: that's true

Tanone: besides he has no money how would he get there, and I doubt he's crazy enough to drive there esp after making threats over the phone when you can have the cops verify that he called you.

Marie: okay...I need to go but thank you so much for all the great info ☺

Tanone: k.. chat you soon, bye

There is it. A true and sordid tale of love found and lost online. My horses' heads remain in tact and my house still stands. Not to say it couldn't of went the other way. There are plenty of nut cases out there that would cross that line. I think it's important that people learn from the conversations and watch for the warning signs when chatting. If you encounter anyone that tries to keep you all to themselves or places any demands on you, especially within days of first meeting you...step back...reconsider. Controlling behavior is dangerous behavior. Also anyone that is ready to tell you they love you before having been face to face with you...has some serious issues. Play safe.

To repeat, neuroses, neurasthenia, psychasthenia, and the various forms of neuropathy and psychopathy are dysgenic factors. But people suffering from these conditions often are among the world's greatest geniuses, have done some of the world's greatest work, and, if we prevented or discouraged marriage among people who are somewhat "abnormal" or "queer," we should deprive the world of some of its greatest men and women. For insanity is allied to genius, and if we were to exterminate all mentally or nervously abnormal people we should at the same time exterminate some of the men and women that have made life worth living.

Woman: Her Sex and Love Life

Feeding A Fetish

Growing up in a strict religious family, miles from the nearest city, I always felt like the ugly duckling. I don't remember how those feelings started but I do have many distinct recollections of childhood traumas that enforced the feelings. Apparently I wasn't a big fan of combing my hair. I remember being forced to go to a little brick house where the lower level had been turned into a beauty parlor. It was always full of little old ladies sitting under enormous helmet like hair dryers and the ozone depleting hairspray mist hung sickeningly in the air. I'd look through magazines full of smiling faces and bouncy curly locks. Then I'd sit almost strapped into the vinyl chair with tears on my cheeks as once again my hair was hacked into an easy-to-care-for bowl shaped do.

The pretty girls would come to school after a new hair cut and show it off to all their friends. I would try to hide in the bathroom, or the back of the classroom, or out on the dodge ball field with the boys, who luckily—between kindergarten and third grade—didn't seem to judge me, or my bad hair. My strongest desire was to go unnoticed and except for occasional finger points and giggles, I did.

How sad, growing up hoping to exist without being acknowledged. I tried to keep my own daughter from ever feeling that way. I made sure she had cute clothes, long hair and the confidence to stand up for herself. She was the most independent little thinker I'd ever met and I was always so proud. I know I pushed to hard at times, but she was never one to hide in the shadows, and I envied her childhood.

Around sixth or seventh grade I started to have a little more confidence in some areas of my life. My artwork always got noticed and I enjoyed playing softball and football at school. It felt good when someone said something nice to or about me and even though I wasn't comfortable with praise I did long for more of it. Physically I still felt like I didn't fit into my own body. I was inches taller than the other girls and most of the boys. I never stood up straight because it made me stand out too much, yet...I remember having a new dress for the Christmas concert my eight-grade year and I needed shoes to go with it, so my family of four headed off to the shoe store.

Mom always picked out the sensible flat shoes for me and I hated them. She was a short woman only five foot three and I towered over her. I think she was busy helping my brother find shoes when I came across the least sensible pair of shoes in the whole store. They had almost four-inch heels, open toes and long leather like strings to tie around the ankles. Plus they were in my size! I eased the box off the shelf and went to the far end of the store to try them on. After sliding my toes under the strap and bending my feet in a way which nature never intended, I grabbed the cold metal frame of the shoe store chair and pushed myself up. I had to throw my shoulders back to keep from falling on my face. Carefully I stepped in front of the tiny foot mirror and was amazed at how pretty my feet looked. The angle of the shoe gave the illusion of them being much smaller than size ten. I took a few steps. I stood tall and straight, and grinning from ear to ear. My balance was better than expected and soon I was able to strut myself to the other end of the shoe store. Dad saw his girl with a happy face. Mom saw the ridiculously inappropriate heels on my feet. Lucky for me, dad and I won that day and I got my heels. I loved them.

*   *   *   *   *

After a couple days of mourning about my east coast experience I was more determined than ever to find the right man for me. I posted a singles ad online. When I uploaded a couple provocative photos of myself I started to get more attention than ever and I loved it! The only bad thing seemed to be the location of most of the men that were interested in me. Germany, Ireland, England, South Africa, Florida, California, New York and once again India (where they worship cows and large redheads). I also turned down the deals from Arabs that offered their first years salaries for getting them into the country. This was before 9/11 and there may not be any connection but I often wonder.

I would often change my posted picture just to gauge the different responses. If it was a cleavage picture all the boob men would find me and leave me such gems as—nice cans! But, what came as a surprise were how many men complemented me after I posted a picture of myself in some heels. I hadn't paid that much attention to my legs, and had felt that they were too big and muscular to be sexy. All the cleaning horse stalls and throwing bales of hay had over developed my calves and I was self-conscious. Now after all the worrying I find out many men love curvy strong legs. HURRAY!

One such man wrote me an email. He described himself as single/41/Chicago, short dark brown hair, blue eyes and five foot ten. It was a brief note just to let me know he was interested. I went to his profile to find more information:

What makes you happy and what makes you sad?
Let's just say that I have a HUGE heart, extremely caring and passionate. I can watch a Jerry Lewis telethon and go thru a lot of Kleenex!
I'd just like to add...
The photo I have posted in my profile is a favorite photo of mine showing a gorgeous pair of women's legs in heels, they are NOT my legs! If you're offended by them oh well. I didn't post them to offend you I posted them cause it's my profile to express MY likes and dislikes. Legs and high heels—short, long or somewhere in between—put my hormones in an uproar and melts me down quickly. I'll be putty in your hands, and that's a wonderful feeling! Oh...if you don't have a picture out here, forget it—I'll probably never make contact with you.

Hmm, a foot fetish guy, I had met other men online that would say they wanted to suck on my toes and I usually hit the ignore button ASAP, this man hadn't said anything about licking, sucking or ejaculating—just that he liked looking. Realizing that I now obviously liked showing I decided to keep an open mind and chat with Nutz4Legz.

I messaged him and found him charming and intelligent. We could talk about many different subjects but the favorites revolved around shoes and legs. I encouraged some of this by taking more photos of my legs and sending them to him. Each time I'd show him a picture he'd reply back, "You are one amazing and beautiful woman, I can't get enough of you...I want to climb through my screen and kiss you."

...and my friends wondered why I loved to be online so much.

We chatted often and exchanged more pictures. He was a good-looking man and I liked his voice when we talked on the phone. I still felt that his leg/foot/shoe fetish made him a bit odd but I was getting over it. I referred to him as, "That foot guy," when chatting with my friends until one day we were chatting and he started to send me web page links to sites that sold shoes. I was so excited I could hardly stay on my chair. So many styles, colors…oh, and leather, satin, suede…<drooling> he was thrilled, I was thrilled and at that moment I realized I too had a fetish, a shoe fetish. He fed into my footwear frenzy by telling me to pick out a few pairs. I hadn't been online a full year yet and I'd received all kinds of offers men never backed up—but this was like circling all the items I desired in the Sears Christmas catalog…I knew I'd never get them but I had fun imagining there was a chance. We spent the entire afternoon swapping links to our favorites. It was quite possibly the most aroused I have ever been…LOL. He requested my shoe size and address. I was hesitant to admit how big my feet were or where I lived because of course this was the weird, "Foot guy," but I admitted in four inch heels I may need a ten and a half and than I gave him my work address. He couldn't have cared less what size I wore he was just as giddy as I was about the shoes themselves.

Just like that I was in love. Blue calfskin, four-inch heels, thigh-high, lace-up-the-front…boots. I swear I could smell them through my computer screen. I couldn't take my eyes off of them. Yes, yes…oh my gawd…yes…I wanted to cuddle up with them in bed, I wanted to top them with a short skirt and strut all over town. Sure—they looked like stripper boots, of course tongues would wag…I was in deep meaningful lust. When I could breath again I pasted the link to my new best friend the shoe appreciation man. He liked the boots but said he was more into shoes. The boots would cover too much of the legs he admired. Two hundred and fifty dollars was also a little more than I think he wanted to spend, yet he said that would be a gift for after we had met face to face. I saved the link to my love in my favorites and reluctantly closed the window.

Nutz4Legz—I'm nuts about you Marie
Marie—I hope you stay that way
Nutz4Legz—This is a first for me…honest…this whole buying shoes and all…WOW! I'm loving it!
Marie—I've never had anyone do this for me, it's very exciting!
Nutz4Legz—plus I know you love to wear them, and you look so awesome in them, I can't lose!
Marie—okay, back to work…take care & talk to you later
Nutz4Legz—Wednesday you will start to receive packages!
Marie—YEAH!!! I am thrilled!

Nutz4Legz—kisses sweetie, til tomorrow?
Marie—okay, kissssssesss b~bye

Amazingly, Wednesday came and so did three of the most incredible pairs of shoes I'd ever seen. The four inch heel open toe blue pumps with ankle strap, the black closed toe with cutout centers to show off my arches, and an impossible-to-walk-in pair of shiny six-inch ankle snappers. I couldn't believe my good fortune. I was beaming (yes I mean smiling although I'm sure my nipples were hard too). OMG, a man from the internet was true to his word! I rushed home to put on some nylons and try on my shoes. I grabbed my digital camera and took a few pictures showing off my legs and the heels. They were such a luxury to me. I could never bring myself to pay over a hundred dollars for one pair and yet here I had three pair each more expensive than any I'd ever purchased for myself.

I sent off a thank you email to my new best friend—the obviously confused yet generous foot fetish man—and I included several photos. Later that night he messaged me and I knew he was just as excited as I was. He told me the three pair from the English company wouldn't arrive for possibly weeks and this time I believed they really were coming.

We continued to get to know each other online and on the phone. He was always a gentleman yet I continued to have some reservations because after all he was a foot-fetish-freak. Eventually the package from England arrived and I held my breath hoping to find my true loves…the blue calfskin boots…he said he hadn't ordered them but I hadn't given up hope. <big sigh> No boots. I opened the box containing the red suede pumps with three sets of straps and buckles…mmmmm…so nice. I smelled them, petted them…auugghh-hhh…my fetish, my freakiness…I obviously had issues, but I also had shoes, expensive, seductive, glorious shoes. I took my new treasures home and had another well received photo shoot. The shoe fetish girl and the foot fetish man, could this be my fate?

Foot guy wanted to fly to Minneapolis to meet me. We hadn't cybered, there had been no phone sex and I imagined in person he'd stare at my feet and make me uncomfortable as the guy in high school that got a little twitchy when someone would slip off their shoe and arch their foot where he could see it. I went to my favorite site to visit my boots. I agreed to pick up the fetish man at the airport. He was flying in for just a few hours so there would be no pressure. I thought it was sweet. I knew he'd be creepy.

Waiting at the gate made me nervous. My nylons were grabbing at my ass and the new shoes were not broke in enough to be comfortable, yet I wanted to wear them to show my appreciation for all the money he'd spent spoiling me.

James the foot fetish man arrived in a black leather trench coat that smelled as sexy as he looked. He gave me a big hug and told me how pretty I was. I melted. I'm sure I kept staring at him amazed at how handsome he was yet wondering when he'd get creepy.

We went to The Mall of America and had dinner at a nice Italian restaurant. Conversation flowed and we spent the rest of the day walking hand and hand around the mall. We shopped for shoes, we shopped for lingerie and I loved his tastes. I didn't let him pay for anything I purchased that day just to show him I wasn't after his money. I let him run his hand up my calf when we stopped to rest on a bench by the giant Snoopy. He kissed me softly and it was very nice.

Time flew and I had to get him back to the airport. We kissed and hugged and I realized the foot fetish freak was really a very nice guy. A gentleman. We remained friends but I never saw him again. I never got my boots either <pout>. I think the distance and our lives were just too different to work long term.

Someday when I have money…I will send him very nice shoes.

> Of what use are warnings to a girl, when under the influence of
> a heavy dinner and a bottle of champagne, to which she is unac-
> customed, her passion is aroused to a degree she has never experi-
> enced before, her will is paralyzed and she yields, though deep
> down in her consciousness something tells her she shouldn't?
>
> Woman: Her Sex and Love Life

Beware the little thumbs

I was pretty burnt on the Internet dating thing after my Rhode Island experience, so I decided to get my ass out of the computer chair and bar hop around
my local area. It was fun telling stories and bull shitting in the bar that evening.
Not only did I have my own crazy experiences to tell but also the stories of all
my new online friends. I also received about a dozen new jokes a day to my
email and not everyone else in the bar lived online so most they hadn't heard. I
was a hit. I also had gained some incredible new flirting skills from all the
online chatting.

Skills may not be a fair description. I was down right bold. It was a new
thing for me and I adapted quickly. I knew how to dance around a subject to
get a man to say whatever I wanted him to say. I had learned what phrases
would make a man weak in the knees. I had been with more than one man...I
wasn't afraid like I used to be. All my months of chatting had given me some
confidence in my appearance. Men from all over the world had told me I was
pretty, beautiful...sexy. I didn't completely believe it yet but I had escaped
from the previous notion that no one would ever want me again.

I scanned the bar hoping to find the only guy from high school that I occasionally still had dreams about. The one who sat behind me in history class
that first day at my new school. The one that asked the guy across from me to
check me out and see if the new girl had big boobs. Damn that girl has been
through a lot. I remember developing so early and being so uncomfortable in
my own skin that I always slouched and tried to hide my figure.
Hiding...slouching...barely speaking...so many years wasted...<sigh> oh
where was that high school heart palpitator now! The girl had grown into
woman and was ready to try some of the things she missed out on. It was disappointing not to find him but I wasn't going to let it get me down. I'd find
someone else to play with.

I'm thinking that I had something low cut on and was showing off the cleavage…umm…—because I almost always do—when an old friend showed up. We hadn't seen each other since I was single. His marriage had also ended so we had a lot to talk about. Nothing too serious, but it was nice to have been through some of the same shit. It was so strange being face-to-face talking. Most of my flirting was done online or on the phone. I chatted so much I could almost see the typed words coming out of people's mouths when they spoke. When something funny was said, laughing was my second response. Typing LOL was the first!!

Whatever topic was started always twisted around to something sexual in meaning, more often than not because I worked it that way. When I was home chatting I got hundreds of photos of men. Men also loved to put on their web cams and show me their "junk". While a man would beg and beg a woman to see revealing pictures, all a woman has to do is ask. Hell, half the time you didn't even have to ask! You got them anyway. Being the curious creature I am, I enjoyed looking…I liked to compare…I desired to find a true method of estimating the size of a man's junk by some other physical feature.

You hear all kinds of comparisons. Wisconsin had already taught me that the size of the man…didn't determine-the size of the man, and Rhode Island had brought a whole new…why does it bend like that query. Months of online research had brought about a thumb theory that I was sharing with the group. While scanning the group I noticed my friend had tucked his into his fists, hmm…not a good sign, but very funny.

We laughed and joked all night. Sporadic thoughts of missing my chat buddies did cross my mind but for tonight I was living IRL (in real life). When the bar closed my friend and I went to an after bar party. I had decided he had gotten sexier since the last time I'd seen him, and…since he was the best looking man out that night…I thought I wouldn't mind taking him home with me. I couldn't decide if he was interested in me or not. I flirted a little more obviously and found excuses to run my hand along his thigh. I offered him a ride back to his truck and on the way he finally kissed me.

He agreed going to my place would be a good idea. I took him to my room. He took charge and kissed my nervousness away. I reached to undo his pants and he wouldn't let me. I lay on my bed enjoying and he kept kissing me as he undid my clothing. I trembled as he kissed his way down my body. With his head between my thighs he devoured me. It was incredible…I couldn't believe how good he made me feel. After I had enough attention to start feeling guilty I wasn't giving any back, I told him it was my turn.

I reached to undo his belt and pants and as I lowered his zipper he said, "beware the little thumbs." We both laughed…and I made a mental note on how accurate my thumb theory was. It's a smart man that knows his weaknesses and learns other skills. The night was great and the next morning I dropped him back off at his truck. He gave me a quick goodbye kiss and I wondered if I'd hear from him again soon. I was proud of myself for not asking or expecting more. We'd had a good time and if that's all it was…that was okay with me.

OMG, Merry Christmas

The Orgasm. The culmination of the act of sexual intercourse is called the orgasm. It is the moment at which the pleasurable sensation is at its highest point, the body experiences a thrill, there is a spasmodic contraction in the genital organs, and there is a secretion of fluid from the genital glands and mucous membranes.

Woman: Her Sex and Love Life

Getting There

Eighteen months without an orgasm seems like enough of a sentence to drive any man or woman insane. The absolute frustration, the tension…it was not for lack of wanting to reach orgasm, I'd had a few partners, some phone sex, some cyber sex, it was just that nothing seemed to get me over that edge. Occasionally I meet a woman that has never in her life had an orgasm, I take the deepest pity on them. Men complain about women not enjoying sex, hmm…if I had never reached orgasm, did not know what I was missing…maybe, just maybe I wouldn't give a damn if I was getting any or not either. But, I did know. I missed the rush, missed the dry mouth, the tingling from head to toe and the calm that settles in after a good explosive session.

Men get caught up in their own skills. Some have mastered the technique needed to get a certain woman to climax and become delusional thinking they have the master key to any woman's orgasm. I hate those guys, LOL. Just because Sally liked her clit flicked or Jessica wanted her nipples about bitten off does not mean it's going to work with me. A good lover starts from the inside of their prospective partner and works their way to the physical.

This brings me to the beauty of cyber and phone sex. It's mental not physical. A great lover is a creative, descriptive, responsive, a great lover gets in your head not just your pants. Over the years I learned the best cyber and phone sex came from connecting with writers and musicians. Is it possible great sex is a right brain kind of thing?! More likely it relates to them being elusive and my dread for predictability. Ouch, self psychoanalyzing hurts…lets move on.

Okay, there I was peering into the glowing box on my desk searching for love and the cure for my orgasm retention syndrome on a single's dating site. Like most people I have a vision in my head of what the man of my life looks like, unfortunately I also have the sound of his voice. Seems a bit nit picky to want both but I do. So I search. I set up my match criteria and name the search pickybiatch. Within seconds I have a list of men just waiting to jump into my reject pile and a few possibilities.

What you might like about Max30ish:
Height: 6'3, 210, non-smoker, well built, totally faithful, very supportive, good sense of humor who's goal is romance/relationship.

Nice start but he lives in Indiana. I don't care and I message him anyway. We get along great and he loves my photos and tells me he is incredibly attracted to me. I like him. He is attentive and kind, he can make a joke and take a joke, he doesn't try to be possessive and I look forward to every minute we get to chat to each other. Within days I give him my phone number and he calls…I hear "the" voice.

I am in awe and hang on every word he utters. Max asks me about my day, my animals, my work and he listens. I am completely in lust with him even though he has no pictures of himself to post online. He's tall, well built, athletic…just what I'd hoped for. The distance becomes a huge obstacle and we wish we could be closer. I explain my mental block on reaching orgasm and he doesn't push the phone sex. I do. Just listening to him has me more worked up than I'd been in a very long time and my imagination has drawn the sexiest man I've ever seen right into my bed. Max is not vulgar he is respectful. Over and over he asks what I want and just as any great fantasy he gives it to me. From his mind to his voice, through my head, to my own fingers he travels to the specific spot that makes me shudder. Max begs me to cum for him and I do!

OMG! Finally! The barrier has been breached, the flood-gates opened and I'm allowed some of the missing pleasure in my life. He is genuinely excited for me and like a kid with a new trick I want to show him again and again what I can do. We talk and play each night before falling asleep and each morning anxiously grab our sticky phones and wake each other up. I'm happy, content, satisfied and still without photographic proof that my new lust exists.

After over a month of me pressuring him to be fair and share photos he decides Polaroid's through snail mail are the easiest way for me to see him. It's a long wait. We keep playing with each other. I get mail. The handwriting is very nice, masculine and neat. I breathe deep and open the letter containing my lover. My heart sinks. It's not him. It's not the man in my head that's spent so many nights in my bed. The man in the pictures has different lips, different eyes, more hair in some places yet less in others than the man that's been in my bed. The man that makes me cum is more sculpted. He's…

When my phone rings I try to suck it up and not sound disappointed. I decide to keep him as a special phone friend since we work so well that way. Only now it doesn't work and he knows it. Even chatting about our days becomes forced and we drift apart.

It's tough getting your fantasy to pick up his phone. If he does, take my advice…never ask for his photographs.

The foundation, the basis of all love is sexual attraction. Without sexual attraction, in greater or lesser degree, there can be no love. Where the former is entirely lacking the latter can have no existence.

Woman: Her Sex and Love Life

Sweet, Sweet Bill

Sometimes the fear of being alone pushes me into a frenzied search to have a man in my life. Society portrays a woman whole when she has a clean house, good kids...and a husband. Just a husband, any husband, any man is better than no man. If he has a good job, security...smiles for strangers on the street...a woman should count herself lucky. If he comes home from his good job and punches holes in the walls while he curses you out for not having the house clean enough...or the food cooked the way he expects it...at least he did come home. Yes, every woman needs a man...society demands it.

Being from a very rural small town area...I knew the man for me didn't happen to live just down the block. I also have this possibly child like belief in fate. Fate had brought me the internet, so I figured I was supposed to be there, online...so the love of my life could find me. I'd also seen a psychic in New York that had enforced my fantasies by telling me that my soul mate would find me there and we would be happy. Maybe you think that is crazy, sad, pathetic...delusional and...maybe I was, but I was a me...not a we, so the search continued.

Wednesday night, Feb. 24th
Tally: Hi Marie
Marie: hello
Tally: how's going
Marie: its good.. and you?
Tally: alright...keeping warm....little tired, where from
Marie: southern MN
Tally: I'm in Michigan w of Detroit
Tally: A/S
Marie: 32/f you?
Tally: 33/m

Marie: cool.. married??? kids??
Tally: what do you do?
Marie: raise paint horses
Tally: single/no kids/accountant (a cool one)
Marie: lol...well my first thought..was.. ohhhh shit...boring...lol
Tally: what do you do w/paint horses
Marie: my stud.. is a reining horse...
Tally: you single
Tally: I rein
Marie: no way..... I'm very single
Tally: kids?
Marie: one daughter...15.. and you?
Tally: I'm still looking for my true love...so I never had any kids like 'em though
Marie: well.... i was 16 when it happened.. i thought i loved the ass.. spent the next 16 years with him even...then...shit hit the fan.. LOL
Tally: Testify baby...lol
Marie: lol...shit happens...
Tally: yeah it helps grow things
Marie: lol........
Tally: been there done that, never kept the ring
Marie: you really rein????????????
Tally: I can rein, very talented
Marie: what kind of horse do you have??
Tally: I don't have a horse, I just rein
Marie: on what type?
Tally: What exactly is reining
Marie: lol....
Tally: lol you caught me
Tally: you like to dance Marie and wrestle
Marie: lol...sure, I'm not a great dancer...but...one hell of a wrestler....
Tally: me too, I'm really a musician and an accountant...love music
Tally: like to wrestle
Marie: lol...what instrument do you play?????
Tally: Sax, piano, and guitar
Tally: what do you look-like
Marie: very cool...I'm going to take guitar lessons.. i play the piano
Marie: 5'10, auburn, teal...long legs.. fair skin...large chest.. and you??

Tally: thats cool....really cool
Tally: 6'1 blonde, 235, brown, broad chest/shoulders...solid
Marie: ohhhhhhh yummmmmmmy
Tally: Yeah I'm still droolin on those legs and I love auburn hair that is soooo beautiful
Marie: lol...well maybe
Tally: I like a woman I can hold on too. I hope I'm not too forward ma'am
Marie: lol.. ma'am.. nice cowboy touch.. lol
Tally: I'm a little bit country and a little bit rock-n-roll
Marie: ohhhh nooooooo...its maries brother.. Donnie...hehehehehe
Tally: born in Detroit but love the country
Tally: no I'm not a Mormon
Marie: moron?? oooopppss.. mormon...lol
Tally: but I have hair and dimples
Marie: OMG...im a sucker for dimples...send pic now.....
Tally: I don't have one to send, do you
Marie: yes.. but.. like to exchange...
Tally: I'm sorry I have to get one to send
Marie: i could send...but.. where????
Tally: The dimples are on both cheeks...very contoured
Tally: *******@msn.com
Marie: mmmmmmmmmmm....
Tally: will you send...Marie...please!
Marie: ok.. im sending.... brb
Tally: I like those mmm's
Marie: ok...here they come...hahahaha
Tally: hope you're not a guy, lol
Marie: eeeewwwwwwwwww that would be nasty
Tally: all right than one moment please
Marie: I've had women chase me here...one wanted to be my first lesbian experience...lmao
Tally: you look so gorgeous
Marie: ohhhhh.... you are too kind
Tally: If I was a lesbian I'd kill for you
Marie: LMAO............. and.. if you were a man...lol
Tally: Oh my gaaaawwwwwd I'm a man and I can't take my eyes off your eyes,
why are you single, you're so beautiful.....the guys must be jerks there

Marie: i don't know…. newly divorced…independent.. sexually demanding.. lol.. you tell me….

Tally: I like to live up to demands, I'm very conscientious. I wish I had a picture for you

Marie: well.. you're intelligent…get one….

Tally: I will. Oh are you busy Friday

Marie: LMAO

Tally: I think I have to tend to some business in MN

Tally: what is LMAO…

Marie: LOL….. well.. i could use your.. expertise

Marie: Laughing My Ass Off

Tally: are you a model?

Marie: oohhh please…. I'm not even pretty

Tally: those eyes are mezmerizing…..and I do mean your eyes….they are piercing even when your laying down. You've got a very beautiful face

Marie: ohhhhhhh i like you……

Tally: and the obvious don't even need to be mentioned

Marie: lol…. you don't mind?

Tally: I would never leave you. Would you like to be my true love, I could wrestle with you and dance!

Marie: mmmmm.. you would have to teach me to dance….

Tally: and you can show me how to wrestle, would you like to dance w/me

Marie: what type of dance???

Tally: I like to dance fast than slow than fast

Marie: lol.. to what kind of music?

Tally: country, rock and the music of Al Green for soul searching

Marie: mmm nice

Tally: you like?

Marie: yes…………..

Marie: so.. how many kids do you plan on having???

Tally: I'd like 2-3, I come from a family of 8, I'm the last

Tally: I thought you were gone..

Marie: disconnected.. sorry, miss me?

Tally: you like making kids

Tally: yes I missed you but I do have your pic

Marie: lol……….

Tally: Can I tell you something?

Marie: sure…

Tally: I got so excited when I saw you....I couldn't help it
Marie: couldn't help what??? hmmmm???
Tally: oh I think I can let your imagination take care of that question....I never had this happen before on this thing
Marie: omg...you sure.....
Tally: Honest
Marie: hmmm.. that pic has had that effect before...
Tally: Nooooo....I want to be the only one....is that being to possessive?
Marie: i like it...
Tally: Wow.....aren't you offended....most women hate that...but I like to protect my Love
Marie: my X...wasn't and that hurt.. I'd rather have possessive
Tally: I'd love to be your one good one, what do you like to do besides horses, dancing and wrestling?
Marie: photography, writing, laughing, games, cards...nature
Tally: you like hiking/camping?
Marie: camping.. is ok...but.. id rather ride than hike...youve seen that load i have to carry.. lol
Tally: Traveling?
Marie: oh yes...i just started to recently.. and i love it
Tally: I'm not ignoring your load but I was interested in you and talking a little
Marie: was???
Tally: Yes, I like to talk and get to know someone
Marie: so what's wrong?
Tally: I'm happy
Tally: you ever been to MI?
Marie: sorry.. got a funny vibe...thought you misunderstood something i said
Tally: no, I like you and hearing about you....you're interesting
Tally: like to give you a huge hug
Marie: mmmmmmmmmmm...thanks
Tally: do you date?
Marie: i might.. lol.. but haven't
Tally: I'd date you
Marie: you would??? that's sweet!
Tally: dance nice and slow and keep you happy
Marie: mmmmmmm...happy...
Tally: you like to snuggle

Marie: mmmmm.. i love touch.. lots and lots of it

Tally: me tooo

Marie: mmmmmmm.. goooood

Tally: I love to run my fingers through that long flowing....auburn hair, those eyes are so sensual and full lips

Marie: mmmmm...wish i could see you

Tally: except w/o the lipstick

Tally: I can be up there in a few hours...lololol

Marie: lol...how would you get here???

Tally: I-94 straight up

Tally: I would melt in your arms, barely able to speak

Marie: ohhhh you are such a smooooth talker

Tally: am I being too rude I like to pay you respect and keep you safe, but I would have to kiss you alot

Marie: i like.. tell me more, mmmmmm.. kisses.. would be great

Tally: I wouldn't make you walk too far I like to ease your load, carefully massage you and take care of you

Marie: mmmm...would you take care of me?

Tally: yes....I would...pamper and bathe you and keep you warm in the cold MN nights

Marie: wowwwwwwwwwwwwwwww

Tally: Could you learn to like that

Marie: it would take some getting used tooooo

Tally: I'm a guy who likes to treat you like a lady not a toy, but we could play together I love to share what I have

Marie: what do you mean by that?

Tally: I'm a very giving person...what's mine is yours

Marie: that's how i always am.. but.. i usually end up with takers...

Tally: noooo..I believe in partnerships. I'd like to hold you really close to me and nibble your neck

Marie: mmmmmm.. i would love that

Tally: and caress you and tell you you're safe and give you a real warm wet passionate kiss

Marie: mmmmmmmmmm..............how wonderful

Tally: run my hands over your body, lick your lips, squeeze you, fall for you and kiss your nipples

Marie: ohhhh...please dooo

Tally: and squeeze your hips and your ass, rolling your nipples into my dimples

Marie: ok.. you don't sound like my accountant...lol

Tally: nuzzling you all over, I can only think of this right now....numbers are for business hours....you're for coming home too, meeting you at the door and kissing you

Marie: ohhhhh god.. i could use you

Tally: and whispering in your ear how much I've wanted you all day

Marie: mmmmmm.... i would have to take you to bed...I'd meet you at the door.. with something sexy and naughty on

Tally: and sharing romantic evenings and building a home while we enjoy our life

Marie: what about my horses?

Tally: what are you wearing

Tally: I love your horses can we ride them

Marie: just jeans...and sweater...nothing fancy.... we could ride...

Tally: Can we picnic in the middle of a field and make love on the meadow

Marie: mmmmmmmmmmmmmmmmmmmmmmmmm, sounds perfect

Tally: dress you up for an evening in the city and have a romantic time together

Marie: I've never ever.. been treated like that

Tally: What r u wearing at the door Honey

Tally: so you'd be bored w/this

Marie: black stilettos...thigh highs.. black.. w/bows...and...black satin thongs...with.. stretchy velvet negligee

Tally: I would love to treat you that way

Tally: oh my gawd, I've never been treated like that

Tally: We won't be bored...nope...no boredoms. I take you in my arms and tell you how gorgeous you are and how much I want you in our bed

Marie: mmmmmm.. i love to keep sex interesting.. wild...hot...fun!!!

Tally: I lick you all over your thighs as I squeeze you all over. No other people please.....is that ok. I just want you

Marie: mmmmmmmm...spoil me..!!

Tally: you wrap your legs around my back as I sip the perspiration off of your inside thighs

Marie: WOWWWWW...you go...wooohoooo

Tally: My spelling will be a little difficult...please forgive me my dear

Marie: mmmmmm......when will you send me a pic of you?

Tally: I reach under the band-leg of your panties and feel your steaming beauty, you are so wet and sooooooo horny

Tally: I'm like really out of my pants....before I strain something
Tally: I kiss your knees and your long legs, nibble and lick the stilletos before I take them off to nibble your toes
Marie: oooohhhhhh...yesssss
Marie: ewww.. not the toes!!!
Tally: I reach into you so I can be inside, caressing and licking you
Marie: mmmmmmm.... yes
Tally: I kiss your cheeks and down around your sexy thighs, I feel you getting hotter
Marie: steeeeeaaaaaammming...i would ache for you
Tally: and I lick all over your nipples as I finger down there
Marie: mmmmm...I'd moan with delight
Tally: kissing your lips and running my tongue in between your mouth, I need to eat you. I start down your bosom
Marie: mmmm...my hands run up and down your back....
Tally: squeezing, licking you, squeezing as I kiss your naval. Your nipples are so big
Tally: I lick your pubic hair and spread you lips w/my long red tongue, I reach inside of you as I nibble and such your wet clit, My face is flooded w/your juices, and I can't stop I roll you on top so you can ride my face
Marie: omg......... mmmmmm...the excitement makes my mouth dry...flecks of light in my eyes.. i almost get dizzzzzzy
Tally: I hold on so tight to our ass. your ass is sooo smooth,
I caress it and try to keep it still as you ride and smash my face with those delicious juices, your thighs are so silky I almost come from all of your excitement
Tally: I love to take care of you
Marie: mmmmmmmmmmm........
Tally: I can see you moaning and writhing up between those delicious thighs you are soooo sexy, I just want you to enjoy! I bite your butt and pinch you as you quiver all over my face, laughing uncontrollable convulsing, I clamp down tight giving you all I can
Marie: mmmmmmm...sounds wonderful
Tally: when you're finished you roll off of me and lay in a spent heap
Marie: mmmmmm...for about.. 10 minutes.. then.. i roll back.. and start playing with you.. begging for more...
Tally: I kiss your lips so sexily and so softly I just love doing that for you. You are so special I can't stop and I'm so hard for you even

when you're just doing dishes or cleaning I always want to grab your ass and play with you

Marie: mmmmmmmm…you make me feel special…ohhhh i would love that!!!! but.. i dont clean.. lol

Tally: ok I'll clean and you can play with me

Marie: ok.. that works

Tally: I'm all for partnerships

Marie: me too and…cleaning ladies..!!!

Tally: but I like to get paid for my domestic talents

Tally: we'll get one

Marie: i have one…

Tally: all right so where was I..

Marie: i was spent.. but.. wanting more

Tally: I roll you over and I climb on top of you

Marie: mmmmmmm…i would love that

Tally: I love the way you look

Tally: We'd have a hitching post in our room

Marie: lmao

Tally: I need you from behind so I can watch your breasts jangle as I enter, don't laugh….that's sexy, I get on top first and I kiss you all over, I need you to take over now

Marie: ok…hang on…

Marie: you are seated on a kitchen chair…no side arms…light is dim…

Tally: atmosphere

Marie: i enter from behind…cover your eyes with a silken cloth

Tally: oh my

Marie: my breasts bump up against the back of your head

Tally: oww

Marie: i move in front of you…

Tally: i can see a little

Marie: well.. i rewrap your eyes.. now you are in complete darkness.. and your other senses take over…your smell.. and touch…. senses.. are.. heightened

Tally: oh yeah, you smell of musk

Marie: i tie your hands behind you too…you cant use them yet you can feel how close i am to you…the heat of my body is sooo close

Tally: mmmmmmmm

Marie: i straddle your chair…i lean in close and lightly run the tip of my tongue.. on your neck

Tally: oooohhh you are so beautiful

Marie: mmmmmm…how can you tell from behind that blindfold????

Tally: i feel it

Marie: lol.. no feeling…except.. with your skin……

Marie: i open your shirt…and rub on your chest…

Tally: you smell sooo good

Marie: mmmmmmm…so do you…i suck on your neck…moving my way to your earlobe…the heat of my breath is on you…warming you….

Marie: i whisper.. i want you…

Tally: me too honey

Marie: i run my hands on your face…over your lips….

Tally: I suck your fingers

Marie: mmm…i kiss you lightly…then…take my finger…feel my self…and bring it back to your lips……

Tally: oh I'm soooo hungry for that taste of you

Marie: i place my finger in your mouth…then….. add my tongue along side of it..

Tally: that is sooo sexy

Marie: i try…lol

Tally: you do

Marie: i continue to lick and kiss you…hot.. wet…and slow…moving down your chest…then following with my finger nails…almost scraping your skin

Tally: I love it! ooohhhhhh my nipples are hard…

Marie: mmmm…tracing circles around them…lightly.. then.. harder…almost pain.. but…soooo much pleasure then.. i follow with my tongue

Marie: down your stomach…licking…nibbling…kissing…hotly…very wet.. noisy kisses with moaning…..

Tally: I want to touch your hair sooo bad

Marie: mmm…you feel it brush against you…but…that's all

Tally: smells so sweet

Marie: i grasp your pants with my teeth.. and pull the button apart, then…the zipper…i use my hands.. and pull them off you…i lick up your calves.. and the insides of your thighs…

Marie: boxers..?? or briefs??

Tally: boxers honey

Marie: mmmmm…nice…i leave them on you yet………..

Tally: nice, lovely, I want you

Marie: mmmmmmm….. i sit on your lap and start to undress my self…

Marie: you can hear it.. but.. can't see, still cant touch me…i talk dirty to you…asking what you would like to do to me…i take off my bra…and.. rub my nipples on your face but i don't let you lick them yet…

Marie: you can feel the heat between my legs…. through your boxers…i stand.. and slip off my panties…

Tally: oh man

Marie: i straddle one of your legs…i almost slide off…..

Marie: you like???

Tally: don't hurt yourself baby untie me so I can hold on to you

Tally: but I love it! I like it so much its blowing my mind

Marie: mmmmmm….. you want to touch me…

Tally: yes, I want you to feel sooo good this is unbelievable

Marie: mmmmm………i first…start to slip off your boxers…

Marie: ooohhhh myyyy….

Tally: oh you're way tooo kind

Marie: mmmmm……. i sit on your lap…i take off your blindfold…and.. kiss you deeply….

Tally: that is so beautiful

Marie: i sit back from you a little…and play with my breasts…circling my fingers around them…like you would like to but cant…

Tally: I really want to

Marie: not yet…i stand.. in front of you….

Tally: I can't but I would ravish you

Marie: I place one foot…on the back of the chair behind your head….

Tally: here we go again!

Marie: and start to trace…the soft lips surrounding my clit with one finger…. while you watch….

Tally: oh my gawd

Marie: would you like to help???

Tally: let me help!

Marie: you cant….

Tally: I need to help

Marie: i laugh at your begging.. but.. decide to give in to you…

Tally: I love to help you

Marie: i sit back on your lap….

Tally: mmmmm those juices

Marie: on the shaft of your cock.. so you can feel me...but.. not enter me...
Tally: I wish I was there this is so cool, I've never done this before
Marie: ok...I'm on your lap..... very close.. reaching around behind you...and.. untying your hands...kissing you again.....
Tally: I have to go to bed....gotta be up at 5 tomorrow I want to talk again real soon and I hope you keep in touch. I really enjoyed this
Marie: well.. leave me then.... you better email me!!!
Tally: I will you've been so good to me I hope you enjoyed it
Marie: i did.. very much
Tally: I think I Love you. Can we get married
Marie: LOL.... well, send me the diamond.. and.. i will decide.. lol
Tally: I'll never be able to sleep now
Marie: write me!!!...
Tally: I will absolutely
Marie: ohhh grab a couple big pillows.. put your face between them.. and.. dream about me
Tally: maybe we can become really close
Marie: yes.. maybe we can!
Tally: I will probably do that. I like MN
Marie: well.. hope you like horses too...
Tally: Its nice up there and you'd be worth every mile
Marie: i will warm a chair up for you.. and we can play this out for real.. if you'd like!?!
Tally: Even if we just talked and who knows. I'd be available this Friday. You want me to come see you
Marie: i have to bowl on friday...lol
Marie: you would???
Tally: sure, I think you'd be really happy and I'd love to make you happy
Marie: wow...what if im an ax murderer..???? lol
Tally: are you? what prison
Marie: LMAO>>!!! cute answer...show no fear..!!! i like that!!!
Tally: NO FEAR!
Marie: lol...okay.. you're making me happy
Tally: Never fear (Bill) is here, thanks!
Marie: well.. good night Bill...go get some sleep!!!
Tally: and this was so much fun.....please be my only one!
Tally: bye Honey
Marie: bye dear!! hugs and kisses...!

It's exciting when you meet someone that thinks you're perfect, exciting but suspicious. I really do have issues with my accountant. He has this big bushy creepy excuse for a mustache and whenever he is attempting to explain anything about my taxes I just zone out on it and find myself watching it go up and down...up and down...up...and...down...never really hearing much of anything he says. That appears to be the only thing I have based my accountant prejudices on...number crunching just bores the hell out of me, but it does show intelligence and that is something important to me this next time around. Bill is also taller than me, which I do like, and he isn't a twig so that takes some pressure off me not being one.

I looked forward to our next chat. It was nice that he was looking for his soul mate and that he had already stated he would be up for living in Minnesota if it came to that, two big points on my—man of my future—chart. The next time I logged on I was pleasantly surprised by a brief email from Bill.

Subject: Re: Marie
Had a wonderful night meeting you, sorry I had to go to sleep, I'm and early riser on the weekdays...take care and write back soon...love me!

I always give huge credit to a man that makes some effort at letting me know he is interested. Bill was definitely on the right track. I sent him a quick note back and an e-card. We chatted again that night.

Marie: hello
Tally: hope i'd find you tonight...loved your letter and cards
Marie: ☺ not as much as i loved yours
Tally: I couldn't get in here the place is packed
Tally: thank you
Marie: i was in a dif room.. it was full so i left in case you couldn't get in!!!
Tally: I can't even type in your pressence
Marie: lol...sure.. sure...
Tally: aww how sweet
Marie: how was your day?
Tally: I was just gonna ask you that, I had a busy one but it was good
Marie: mine was ok...i ran away last night and drove like hell to a casino.. lost a bunch of money.. and came back...lol. Today was ok.. i have lots to do yet

Tally: I signed for a home improvement loan, finalized feb's numbers and made up w/a co-worker
Marie: aaawwww.. how special.. unless she's a hot coworker than...sorry to hear it..
Tally: you ran away, should a came to me
Marie: I'm working on a loan too
Tally: we have Casinos in Detroit
Marie: that would have been a long drive but, I'm sure worth it
Tally: I'd meet you half way
Marie: you wont just fly here to meet me?
Tally: what are you doing tonight
Tally: sure—when
Marie: when would you?
Tally: isn't Mankato where little house on the prairie is
Marie: it's west of my place but not far
Tally: I would fly to see you...who wouldn't
Marie: aaawwww...how sweet of you when you going to send me a pic?
Tally: Did I tell you how much I missed you yet! Kisses n hugs
Marie: aaaawwwww ty hun...been thinking about you a lot too
Tally: I'm gonna send you me
Marie: mmm.. in the flesh huh??
Tally: uh huh, pictures don't do me justice
Marie: lol.. I'm sure they do
Tally: Love those eyes...so sparkly
Marie: i look like hell in mine too
Tally: Nooo bite your tongue...or you can bite mine
Marie: well.. that one is good for me.. you'd be disappointed in person, you are way to sweeeeeet for me
Tally: I'd love to whisper in your ear and hug you so close. I was on air, Part of a great day—couldn't ask for more unless you were right here w/me now Sugar
Marie: ☺
Tally: nice smile and good stems lol
Marie: lol...you are great!!!
Tally: So'd you lose all your money
Marie: it was awful!!! $200.. in about 30 min
Tally: Wowwwwww...on what...slots?
Marie: it was bad.. no black jack..
Tally: ohhh geez that's the best odds

Marie: wizard from the room met me there.. he lost that much too..
LOL...we both sucked! i usually have good luck at that...well.. either i
do or i don't.. last night was a don't....
Tally: Wizard?
Marie: yeah...he is in the room just a friend...not a good friend.. i
think he is bad luck! LOL
Tally: of course
Marie: wish you lived close.. ida saved the $$$.. and drove to your
house
Tally: I was getting jealous
Marie: mmm.... could a stuck the hundreds in your pants.. what kind
a dance would that get me????
Marie: no need...i was thinking about you
Tally: I'd have to lamboda you
Marie: ohh baby
Tally: hold me, hold on to me, oh yeah
Marie: mmmmmmm.... sounds good to me
Tally: I wish I was there w/you
Marie: what would you be doing?
Tally: I'd rock you in my arms and kiss you ssoooo deeply on your
poutty lips
Marie: lol...if you were close.. i wouldn't be pouting anymore
Tally: running my fingers through your soft hair, mmmmmm
Marie: mmmmm.. i wouldn't get sick of that...ever...
Tally: kiss your neck and shoulders, caress your cheeks
Marie: ohhh yessss, I would love that...I'd never get tired of it
Tally: hold you when we're through and just melt w/you, kissing
you and holding your hand...mmmmm
Marie: aaaawwwwwww.. i need that sooooo bad
Tally: wake up and just never want to leave each other
Marie: mmmmmmmmmmmmmmmmmmmmmmm yesss
Tally: golden light on your auburn hair you're a goddess like fire
and clouds
Marie: ohh you are soo special.. you can't be real...
Tally: I always wanted to be this way...suspended from reality
w/my woman
Marie: mmmm.. you set me up so high.. i will take a terrible fall
Tally: just a thought I have a vivid imagination
Marie: yes.. and it's wonderful, i just wouldn't want you to be disap-
pointed in my reality. what are you thinking?? right now?

Tally: you speak so beautifully, and you have so many awesome ideas I'm thinking if this is real I don't want to stay in Michigan anymore

Marie: damn, you seem to be what i have always dreamt of but what about your family

Tally: I live on my own

Marie: but.. brothers.. sisters…etc…

Tally: family is always here, they want me to be happy, I've worked hard and tried to be a good person and I feel the karma is strong

Marie: me tooo…

Tally: I don't do this with anybody

Marie: its like you're pulling my heart through my chest right into the screen

Tally: ditto. I really like this, I look forward to you

Marie: wow…i don't know what to say…its scarin me a little..

Tally: We'd know if it was right or not I think

Marie: i don't know.. like i said.. i don't trust myself anymore.. I've been wrong…..

Tally: If you want me I would be there if you didn't than I 'd know it wasn't meant to be I WOULD NOT upset your life or you're responsibilities

Marie: you seem so wonderful.. and the thought that you would come to me is incredible…

Tally: I really wasn't trying to find you, it just happened

Marie: i really like that about this…

Tally: me too

Marie: you don't think I'm nuts because i want to believe in what the psychic told me

Tally: No universal energy gets channeled, I've been alone for awhile and I know what I want

Marie: r u a cpa?

Tally: I'll know if you're her

Tally: no

Tally: I live within my means, I have a good car a nice home and I have a safety net for a rainy day

Marie: i might drive you nuts…lol…i live more for the day…since my parents deaths

Tally: I like money, I like what I can do with it, I like security. I like to travel, buy nice quality things, and I know where it is

Marie: me too.. but i have all that I've wanted.. except for someone to share it with. i would love to travel more but…how could we do that with the two little boys???
Tally: they go too
Marie: ☺
Tally: I don't want your money don't need it
Marie: I'm not worried about that.. that's not what i was getting at
Tally: I'm a self-made man
Marie: it's just the part of the psychic thing that doesn't match perfectly but.. gee she couldn't be completely right.. right?
Tally: what's that
Marie: she said.. he would find me.. and he wouldn't have much money….
Tally: is 60k alot?
Marie: around here it would be.. but.. naaawww…lets say no, you are perfect
Tally: I'm not perfect
Marie: why do you say that?
Tally: I get stubborn sometimes
Marie: lol…ooohhhhh not like me
Tally: I don't lose my temper too easily though, I got a long fuse I am patient
Marie: me either but when i do…omg………….
Tally: same here
Marie: lol…
Tally: I like to listen more than talk
Marie: i don't walk away from an argument.. i want it all out and over
Tally: me too I hate games…just SAY IT
Marie: don't go to sleep until its worked out
Marie: YES!!!!
Tally: Things can be worked out if we want them too
Marie: right
Tally: want the kids to see love in the house not a bunch of phony business
Marie: very true
Tally: They'll know mom and dad fight but they always make up
Marie: you're gonna make me cry…
Tally: and it's never their fault (hug) its all right I like you
Marie: what is there about you that isn't perfect???
Tally: I'm selfish sometimes

Marie: how so?

Tally: like to do things my way

Marie: me toooo

Tally: but I can compromise

Marie: but.. it will still bug you if you would have done it different???

Tally: just don't breathe down my neck. yes, I confess it would

Marie: same here

Tally: I'd trust you to do things you're way if I seen your work

Marie: same here

Tally: I would just move on to something else

Marie: but.. you put the toilet paper roll on the wrong way.. and I'm flippin it back...

Tally: I'm thorough

Tally: We have our own bathrooms don't we, his and hers

Marie: well.. not until you build me a new house

Tally: ok. at least your own sink

Marie: my bathroom is...20x10...12 feet of counter space shower for two...tub for two...always wanted someone to share it all with

Tally: I don't plan on losing everything I have if I get together w/you, I plan on adding to it for us. I need to work, I really like what I do, I need to accomplish

Marie: that's great...

Tally: I want to be a CMA—Certified Management Accountant, its a corporate CPA

Marie: do you need more school for that?? classes?? i live in the sticks hun, maybe you'd hate it here

Tally: no just time to study, I'm doing it now how far from the city?

Marie: which city??

Tally: the biggest one closest

Marie: mankato.. college town.. 30 miles

Tally: Can I tell you something?

Marie: anything! youre killin me.. ask.. please

Tally: My psychic told me I would meet someone that would ease my burden and make my life more fun without always being so worried about work and having to make all the money, but I was told it would just ease my burden, not that I wouldn't be a successful. Is that scary

Marie: i love it

Tally: she has auburn hair and I would drop everything for her

Marie: if i wouldn't of had to pay off my X.. or.. didn't want to add things to my place.. i would have no debt

Tally: things work out, I only have a mortgage

Marie: it's supposed to last forever…true happiness with my soul mate

Tally: I'm suppose to be the happiest I could ever be

Marie: same here

Tally: She's suppose to be my rock and soul mate, this was in Salem Mass

Marie: i would take care of you.. defend you…not let anyone hurt you

Tally: Same here

Marie: do all i can to make your dreams come true

Tally: our dreams

Marie: are your eyes watering?

Tally: I want to believe this is what she said would happen. I'm barely breathing, lost all track of time

Marie: same here

Tally: the other part…she said I would date a blonde but it was only temporary

Marie: ok….

Tally: I just had a short relationship with her we just weren't right for each other

Marie: its over?

Tally: I went out for the last time last Thursday, it was so weird

Marie: why?

Tally: Cause I wasn't even thinking about it and we were talking about life and she was into seeing a lot of other people and we were deciding if we should take it further

Marie: please.. go on..

Tally: She wasn't into the same things I wanted, but it was just no connection, we didn't leave on bad terms its just I know who I'm looking for. Than a few days I felt really free gain

Marie: and now?

Tally: and I wasn't even thinking about the psychic thing

Tally: well we started talking, I thought you were just gone

Marie: I've thought about it a lot…ignored it a couple times.. but still thought about it.

Tally: I was surprised at my reaction to your pic

Marie:???

Tally: I really couldn't take my eyes off you I showed you to my friends and I never would do that

Marie: that's why i wish so badly i had one of you to look at…i feel like i could know.. if i saw you

Tally: I can send one to you

Marie: awww…thats sweet…do they think your insane

Tally: I want to

Marie: please do

Tally: No, I never even thought about it like that. You looked like…like perfect

Marie: ohhh i wish i was

Tally: what's wrong with you?

Marie: I'm too big.. too heavy…. just not pretty

Tally: Honey you are so pretty your face is like nothing I've ever seen before

Marie: you are sooo sweet to me…<tears running down face>

Tally: I know you think everybody sees your boobs and that's it but I swear your eyes were so lovely I couldn't…I was speechless. I was expecting an ugly picture

Marie: lol…and why?? ugly..

Tally: and nothing special, because I'm a pessimist, but when I opened that thing I was just…agog

Marie: lol…I've told my friends you must be a mutant because you're so damn perfect every other way.. LOL

Tally: I thought I was crazy

Tally: cool, lol, I'm a cute mutant

Marie: lol…wheeewwwww

Tally: sigh

Marie: i took my laptop to work today…just so i could keep peaking to see if you'd sent me anymore mail..

Marie: aaahhhh.. i know what you mean

Tally: this is the 1st breath I took since I found you tonight

Marie: my heart skipped when your name flashed on the screen you were the only one i was looking for

Tally: I just want to find you and stop this crazy thing…stop this CRAZY thing called life

Marie: lol, so…when you going to call me?

Tally: I want to

Marie: lol…when

Tally: when you're ready

Marie: do you have an idea in your mind.. of what i would sound like? or. what you hope i would sound like?
Tally: no
Tally: maybe
Marie: yeah...you do
Tally: soft a little deep, breathy...Close?
Marie: lol.. I've been told i should have my own 900 number...lol
Tally: You're a work of art
Marie: lmao
Marie: I've also been told i sound like a six year old.. LOL.. but.. he was teasing me....
Tally: I can act like that sometimes
Marie: that's ok...id rather have silly than stuffy...i want fun!!!!
Tally: Can I call you tomorrow night
Marie: i would love you too
Tally: me too
Marie: omg.. I'm soo nervous already
Tally: it is written. thank you
Marie: kisses...all over.....
Tally: I think sooo who could help it
Marie: do you need to go now?
Tally: its 12:15
Marie: i know
Tally: I need to sleep...with you
Marie: mmmmmmmmmmmmmmmmmmmmmmmm...we wouldn't sleep
Tally: I can't wait til tomorrow but I want to
Tally: ok hon
Marie: ok...
Marie: i don't want to let go of the keyboard
Tally: I really want to wait for you...sooo unlike me...i'm sooo impatient sometimes
Tally: Good night than
Marie: nooooo not yet
Tally: I need to get some air
Tally: ok
Marie: okay...
Marie: look up at the sky.. and i will do the same
Tally: you make me so happy
Tally: ok
Marie: i hope i can

Marie: kiss good night hun
Tally: long kiss good night and holding you in spirit until tomorrow
Tally: what time is good
Marie: what time tomorrow?
Tally: 9 your time
Marie: you tell me. Okay, don't expect it to be a short call ok?
Tally: ok nine than night sweetie I love you
Marie: mmmmm...I'm dying to hear your voice!!
Tally: me too
Marie: amber sounds like me.. so.. make sure its me!!
Tally: I've never done this on line before
Marie: done what??
Tally: I will
Tally: Called anyone
Marie: well.. i hope I'm worth the wait
Tally: I' never thought I'd actually call anyone on line
Tally: I think you are. Good night dear
Marie: i have done it...but haven't heard whatever it is that i need to hear yet
Marie: goodnight hun until tomorrow...i will have you with me every second
Tally:...peace....good karma and tomorrow...bye my dear
Marie: b~bye
Tally: Noooooooooooooooooooooo not good bye, good nite

It's an amazing feeling when you connect with someone online. People everywhere are typically more alike than not...but it's when you find someone that brings to the surface all your hopes of true love and romance...<sigh> it's an amazing thing. I chatted with my girlfriends and told them all about Bill. They were happy for me and wished me the best. The next day dragged while I nervously awaited his phone call. I imagined his voice warm and deep, deep like the man I had been chatting. The kind of voice that would soothe me...mmmmm...I kept checking the clocks.

When the phone finally did ring I could barely get myself to pick it up. It was Bill. It was not however, the voice from my imagination. We talked and got along well. He was sweet and kind, intelligent...and could make me laugh. I chose to ignore my gut, which kept telling me it was not the voice of the right man for me. Every day we made at least one form of contact—emails, phone calls or chatting—I hadn't even seen his picture yet!

Subject: Thank you! Inspirationally and emotionally hooked on you!
Hi Marie,
Can't stop thinking about all the things we talked about this morning, you really moved me. I wished you were here whispering all your dreams in my ear and planning how to get all these marvelous things done. You would truly be someone I could fall in love with, we have so much in common and you're very deep. I want to talk more and more...so if you really want to keep in touch I would love it. I'm a steady guy, no games, just love life and want someone with the kind of imagination that inspires great things together. You're really sweet and nobody should take advantage of that. I would protect you and keep you loved and appreciated...you sound too good to be true but I have faith that people like you really do exist if sought out. Be careful out there honey and don't take any more shit from anyone you are truly a godsend...I like this!
Love,
Bill

How could any lonely woman resist an attentive caring man like Bill. I think he sensed that I had pulled back a bit after our phone conversations and that spurred the flurry of emails and e-cards. I kept an open heart and enjoyed talking to him. Finally, about ten days after our first meeting, he had a picture of himself to send me. Waiting to hear a voice on the phone cannot compare to the wait for a photo to download. You sit there at your computer watching the file transfer percentage...heart beating faster...praying the image that's coming doesn't make you regret all the kind words you've shared with a faceless stranger.

He warned me they were not quality photos, and they weren't. One showed Bill all decked out in a tux, holding a microphone at a wedding reception. The tux was black and the lighting was bad on the picture but I could see he had more of a baby face than I had expected which was fine because it kept him younger looking than he was. The second photo was of him the morning after the big wedding party. It was one of those photos that should have been destroyed right after it was picked up from developing...LOL. Bad hair, eyes squinting closed and a big wrinkly shirt that made him look heavy.

I'm always searching for the good so when put on the spot after receiving a less than flattering photo of someone I have a few standard responses:

Nice Pic ☺ = good quality photo, like the lighting...too bad you look like crap.
Wow, you look great! = I honestly think you're hot enough to sleep with.
You look good ☺ = You look better than 50% of the dorks that send me their pics but I would never sleep with you.
I like your lips (or eyes, or smile or some other distinctive body part) = I had to study your picture until I could find something not repulsive about you.
Wow, check out those muscles! = You poor anal freak, anyone that works out that much is obviously too into himself to be into me and therefore not worth my time.

I stared at my screen trying to decide what to say, after a brief pause I told Bill how much I liked his nice full lips. He was glad I liked the pictures and started asking when he could come and see me in person. I felt bad for being shallow and disappointed over what I saw, but I too have some poor pictures of myself that would leave most men running, I just don't happen to send them to anyone I am interested in. I disappeared for a day and then left Bill an email.

Subject: Hello Bill!
Hello Bill,
Sorry this letter is a day late...I really enjoyed what you sent me last night. Maybe you have missed your calling and should be a writer rather than an accountant!!! I'm at work yet now...thought I would be home by now but the dentist took 2 hours torturing me this morning. I feel awful! Everything hurts and I can't even bite together, I really don't want to feel like this when we meet so please be patient with me. Yesterday I had problems with my stud and ended up getting kicked which was actually a good lesson for me because nothing is broken and maybe I will be more careful next time. I will write you more when I get home, I just didn't want you to worry that I'm not still thinking about you! Take Care, Talk to you soon, Marie

Subject: Re: Hello Bill!
I can't believe a stud would ever kick you, good thing I'm not considered a stud (laugh) but good to hear your pain is all coming to an end, I will talk to you tonight hopefully. Thanks for writing. Today I am enjoying a well deserved afternoon off so I am taking full advantage of the situation and doing nothing for a change. I wasn't gonna even check the e-mail but I was hoping I'd hear from you

the "special one" low and behold like magic as always, thank you my dear.
Wish I could take your pain away...bye for now! Bill

Subject: Salutations
Good Evening,
I hope that if this message finds you it finds you well and that you are having a great evening. If you've read this far you're probably still interested in getting to know each other and that is all the more worthwhile.
I so much enjoy hearing your voice and learning about your life that I feel I know you in such a short time. The coincidence and circumstance of our meeting has kept a constant smile on my face and I'm glad we "bumped" into each other.
When we're speaking or chatting I get so lost in the moment that I don't wish to think of anything else, I couldn't wait to send you my pic so that you could put a face to all these words. I am looking forward to meeting you when you feel the time is right after all I have a bit of old ways in me and I prefer to take it slow and easy and not waste any time at all getting to know you. Whether this is inspired by a psychic in New York or Salem it doesn't matter, whether your teeth are perfect or you feel a few pounds heavy or whatever it doesn't matter to me.
What does matter is that you seem to be the other half of the great mind and soul I've been hoping to find my whole life, the one I always feel may have gotten away in a less mature state of life and I'm relieved that you may be the chance I've hoped would com around again when I was really ready.
Without rushing I look forward to knowing more and more about you as we continue this journey. It's amazing so far and I don't wish to miss another minute on indecision. So please take your time and keep me in mind and let me know when I can wrap my arms around you and give you a great big hug and feel the energy that I feel on this screen and on the phone and in spirit knowing that a mysterious part of my life awaits in a land far away.
Take care and sweet dreams...xoxoxoxoxoxox! Me!

Subject: Evening/Morning
Just wanted to say goodnight. Hope to talk soon. Feels right so far. Enjoy our time together through the wires, don't know why I found you, glad I have its happiness on my heart that draws me to you.
Happiness is a good thing, healing someone you care about is a good thing. Pain in waiting I was told is a good thing also and it brings us something to look forward to as we go through our daily chores and tasks.
So let the minutes and the hours and the days pass by towards earning and accomplishment so I can meet happiness in Minnesota and on common ground and see the journey is a good one. Goodnight Marie...
Bill

Subject: Happy Sunday
Good Afternoon Bill,
I must say your incredibly warm letters seem to be melting the walls of ice surrounding my heart. I try to be the cold and in control person to often I fear. Well.. okay maybe not cold but cautious. I am afraid of being hurt and like I said I seem to have a tendency to fall for assholes and idiots and I already know you are neither.
I admit to being very scared/nervous to meet you. My friends feel that either I am not ready or that I actually care! They are dying for me to meet you so I can let them know what happens.
I also want to warn you about my recent trend for picking men apart and finding something wrong with each one...LOL...well...of course there is but, etc...LOL...geezzzzz. I know I'm far from perfect. Upon reviewing the past months of my life I have realized that since getting rid of my blondish hubby I have avoided all fair haired men like the plague...I started thinking and realized that even all my chat buddies are dark...this wasn't done intentionally but apparently on a subconscious level. Okay...forgive me...I'm rambling.. just be patient with me...yeah...that's what I'm trying to say ☺
Okay...once again please forgive my incredibly strange writing today. I will write more or try calling you later.
Take Care, Marie

Subject: Re: Happy Sunday
Uh hum,
FIRST OF ALL...oh sorry I'm shouting...1st of all my hair is closer to brown than blonde...2nd its all here on my head not in the drain or somewhere in the Detroit River, 3rd I am not from your past I am here now and I am a lil scared too but I do care an I haven't been this happy in ages!
So my friend be critical and be nervous but for christs sakes don't be afraid of me or the things I stand for, flaws happen, those are the beautiful things that happen by accident and you'll either find them endearing or not...you won't know and I won't know until we get to know each other. And on no technicality do I intend to stop writing, calling and hopefully eventually seeing you unless you say stop, because I do care and I like you.
Please let somebody be nice to you...I want that too, life is short and I intend to find just that. You're pretty, very intelligent and if you must know, interesting as hell.
That's all I have to say. Talk to you later...peace and love, Bill

Bless that man for trying and not giving up on me. I knew I was pushing him away. Whether it was from gut instinct because of his voice or photos, or something inside of me that was not yet ready to become involved, I didn't know. I was making excuses and he was not going to play that game. Three hours later that same night I received another email.

Subject: Re: Exciting Happy Sunday and week to come
Marie,
Due to your undying need to avoid any contact with anything remotely good in your love life I have taken the initiative and decided to visit you my dear.
Doo doo doo dooo doot...hold on...I'm comin...hold on I'm comin! A little Motown to get you in the mood, LOL...did I mention I'm black? Hahahahahaha
Anyway,
Yes I will be arriving in Minneapolis/St Paul on the 18th at 11am your time...I have a reservation at the nearby International Hotel. We'll talk later on Monday night to see how we want to work this...I'd hate to make you get up too early and the hotel has a shuttle to/from the airport so we'll see how you feel.

I got a suite just in case you dump me and I have to find someone quick to impress...hahaha...plus I enjoy being comfortable when I travel...I anticipate this adventure with excitement and cannot wait to meet you in person. I will make sure to leave my coke-bottle glasses home so your teeth will not be magnifies as a courteousy to your current (unnecessary) complex...good night my dear, talk to you later...hugs and kisses,
Peace and Love,
Bill

I panicked as I read the letter. He really was coming to see me. I rushed to find my online friends and ask them what they thought. Most of them had read some of Bill's letters to me and were pushing me to let him come see me. This last letter from him only confirmed in their minds that he could be the right man for me. I sent him a sweet e-card letting him know I liked him and appreciated him taking his time and money to come meet me. He of course wrote me back.

Subject: Re: when I think of you from Marie
Hi, got your message. Just getting in from work...happy to hear from you!
Its about 6:45 here...long day went in at 5:30 this morning, never even stopped for lunch, but things are pretty good...slowing down after the big audit and year end business...thank god!
The game was fun last night. Everyone wishes you were coming here so they could meet you. Ha...I told them that I had to check you out first...actually I just want you all to myself honey.
Anywho, I hope we can talk later tonight, missed you yesterday. I stay up until about midnight so I'll try you around 11:30, you can call me anytime you want, looking forward to it!
"The world is a safe and happy place when you care so much about being there whether in spirit or all together, things just work out and the sun always shines on us."
Peace and Love—Me!

Subject: Hi there ☺
I need to head to bed soon but wanted to leave you another message. Its an interesting feeling filled with fear and anticipation when one senses he will be meeting a soul of like mind and caring heart. You come to my life full of fun ideas and beautiful words and

the ease of leaving the bad things behind. Although I keep my anticipation in check for some type of reality it is so much fun planning my visit with you. The most dreaded of days (Monday) has come and gone so easily and I really love feeling all this happiness that you've generated in my heart.
Thank you,
Bill

We talked on the phone the rest of the week. Part of me wanted to get him to cancel his trip and part hoped that meeting him face-to-face would get rid of my fears. I promised to pick him up at the airport and spend the day with him. He was only staying one night and than flying back. He didn't expect me to stay the night and I appreciated him not pressuring me. Of course he hoped I would stay and just in case things went well I did pack an over night bag.

I made sure I got to the airport early. Then I once again had plenty of time to over think everything Bill and I had ever chatted or talked about. I wished I had run late. I had dressed casually and now wondered if my blue jeans and blouse were nice enough for him. I went to the bathroom and fussed over my face…more makeup…less makeup…damn I was nervous. The plane arrived and taxied to the gate with the swiftness of a snail. I remained seated, flipping through a magazine, pretending to read and not be nervous. Passengers began to appear…the angle of the ramp allowed me to see the tops of their heads first. My heart stopped every time I suspected it was Bills light brown mop. A couple times I questioned which of the six foot something light brown haired men was my Bill. When I noticed the baby faced man carrying the roses I knew for sure it was him. Not because of the roses exactly, but more because he was not what I thought of as my type. Besides roses, he carried about sixty pounds more than I expected, and that was all in his butt and thighs. I remembered how I'd never seen a full body picture of him. I was frozen in my plastic airport chair. I wondered if I looked like my pictures. I considered saying I wasn't Marie. I felt like such a shallow shit.

Bill approached me beaming from ear to ear and I got up and gave him a big hug. I thanked him for the flowers and asked about his flight. He told me how great it was to finally be next to me, and I thought about how I really didn't like his voice. We walked to the parking ramp more like brother and sister than soul mates. He gave me another hug as we loaded his bag in my truck. I avoided eye and lip contact. He didn't seem to notice, or just blamed my reactions on being nervous.

I had a few sight seeing type activities for us to choose from for our day. It was so nice to have someone open to new things. We weren't limited to a truck rally or dirt bike exhibition. This man had some culture and it was a nice change. There was a Star Wars exhibit at the museum and we were both excited about seeing it. I figured some art…and some sci-fi geek stuff would be a great blend. Luke Skywalker had after all been my first crush!

Bill impressed me with his knowledge of art. He knew the difference between the impressionists and the realists, and he had a genuine appreciation for many different styles. I kept thinking how nice it was to have someone with similar interests. I tried to ignore the little voice in my head that kept telling me he was not my type, but when he'd try to walk with me holding my hand all I could do was look for reasons not to be holding his. I was just not physically attracted to him and the more I tried to talk myself into him, the more physical things I found not to like about him. We spent hours at the museum. I found myself interested in whatever piece he wasn't near. That way we were kind of together but…not too together.

The stress was beginning to eat away at me and I was making myself sick. Bill suggested maybe getting something to eat would make me feel better and I agreed. He picked out a nice Mexican restaurant and the food was great, but it couldn't make me feel much better. This man had written so sweetly and had spent his own money to come and see me, I felt bad. We went to check him in at his hotel. He knew I wasn't feeling well and suggested just going some place quiet for a bit. I stood about eight feet from Bill as he checked in to his hotel. The clerk behind the desk sensed that we weren't having a very good love connection and announced that he was without charge bumping us up to the Honeymoon Suite. I almost puked.

The room was gorgeous. Mirror paneled walls around a Jacuzzi tub and a king sized bed. All I could think about was what a waste it all was, and about how much fun I could have in a room like that with someone whose bones I wanted to jump. I told Bill I was sorry for not feeling well and laid down on top of the bed. He turned up the air conditioning for me and lay on the far side of the bed. I concentrated on my breathing and tried to tell myself I was feeling better.

After what seemed like only a few minutes I felt Bill roll over closer to me. He put his arm around me and kissed the back of my head. I wanted to leave. I turned toward him to make an excuse and he kissed me. I tried to kiss him back and found myself giggling nervously. Not that cute oh my god I like you giggle…but that…help me, help me I'm so uncomfortable I can't speak laugh. Bill was not aware of the difference. He kissed me again. I pulled away. I told him I was sorry but I really had leave. I didn't feel well, Amber was home alone and the horses needed me…I really had to go.

Poor Bill lost his composure and tried to get me to stay. I told him again how sorry I was but this just wasn't going to happen. I headed for the door and he followed. I said goodbye and he asked why I couldn't just use him for sex like I had the last guy. I paused and looked at him but had nothing to say. I left him crying in the honeymoon suite. I felt like a bad person.

I got in my truck and was relieved to be heading home. I kept thinking how I should have listened to my gut from the start when it said Bill wasn't the right one. I realized how someone liking me was not enough reason for me to like them. I didn't owe that person anything but honesty. I was proud of myself for not staying the night with Bill just to ease some of my guilt. I knew that wouldn't have been a good thing for either of us. Bill was a good man, just not my good man…I'm sure he'd understand that eventually.

Mental or Psychic Masturbation. Some girls and women will abstain from handling themselves with their hands (manual masturbation), but will practice what we call mental masturbation. That is, they will concentrate their minds on the opposite sex, will picture to themselves various lascivious scenes, until they feel "satisfied." This method is extremely injurious and exhausting and is very likely to lead to neurasthenia and a nervous breakdown. You should break yourself of it, by all means, if you can. For it is even more injurious than the regular habit.

Woman: Her Sex and Love Life

Panties on the Wall

One of the greatest things about online chat is that when you want it to be your fantasy world it can be. Especially if you are lucky enough to bump into a like-minded creative person who has some of the same tastes as you do. I don't remember what room Dennis and I bumped into each other in, but I'm sure glad we did. The following session with him was like stepping into an instant mini vacation. We did things I've often fantasized about and I pushed some of my boundaries that in person I'd of held back from experiencing.

Dennis says: hello there
Marie says: hi hun, how are you today?
D: good did I catch you at a bad time?
M: nope just writing a letter
D: ok—let me know when you're finished and if you care to play a little
M: mmmmm…I could use some of that…brb
D: no problem
D: ☺ you ready for a play session?
M: sure baby you mind starting
D: what type of role-play would you care to explore?
M: up to you
D: how about the dom F we talked about a week ago?
M: I don't think I'm up to that today hun, I think I'd rather be taken advantage of if you don't mind…??

D: hmmm options are 1) bar pickup 2) sexetary 3) rape 4) sub-missive F—please choose

M: 1

D: okay background Mardi Gras

D: I'm wearing jeans a polo shirt and holding some good beads

M: I am in a red dress, slit high up the thighs, buttoned down to my belly button with red pumps, wild hair and shockingly red lips.

D: I walk into the streets with some friends, hurricane in my hand and we run into you and a girlfriend in front of a bar.

M: I look right into you eyes.

D: We've been drinking and we hoot at the two of you to "show us your tits"

M: I grab my dress and pull it open to the sides, I say, "Oh baby what would you do with these?"

D: My buddy and I cheer as I slur out something about running my hard one up between them, than we hand over the beads and ask you to share a drink with us

M: I take the beads, put them around my neck and wrap the long strands under my breasts and walk up to you. I take your hand and kiss you fingers.

D: I offer you another string of beads and slide my hands inside your dress carefully tucking them away

M: mmmmmm…I tingle with excitement…I think you are sooooo hot, I want you to touch me again

D: I press my advances and kiss you deep, hoping my buddy is taking care of your girlfriend.

M: I don't care about them, I just want you and I don't care who sees us

D: the bar is packed full of others groping and fondling, I grab our drinks from the bartender and pull you into the crowd

M: I don't even ask your name, I don't want to know it, I just want to feel you

D: We dance tightly against each other as the floor is just packed

M: I breathe in deeply, the smell of you…its like I have an animalistic need to have you and I push myself into you, one leg between yours, rubbing into your crotch, I feel your excitement.

D: my hands clench your dress and pull it up slowly revealing your stockings

M: I'm so glad I wore the fancy panties

D: I pull your dress up to your waist and expose your ass but everyone else is to preoccupied with their own partying to notice it. We kiss deeply. You feel a cold metal against your thigh, I have pulled out a small knife and cut the waist strap of your panties

M: I bite your neck, moaning…breathing hard…we kiss with more passion and lust than I have ever felt. I'm scared but excited

D: I pull them free as a small cheer goes up in the close crowd

M: throwing my head back I scream with ecstasy

D: putting them to my nose I smell your scent

M: I reach for your pants and fumble as I try to get them off of you

D: I yell at the bartender and throw him your panties as a big cheer goes up and he catches them—then steps up and staples them to the wall joining the other trophies for the night.

M: ohhhhh I don't care who sees…you are all I know…all I taste…all I smell

D: smiling at you wickedly I tell you I had always wanted to do that

M: I laugh devilishly and look deeply into your eyes, I've always wanted someone to take me…I want more

D: I tug you after me as we enter the men's bathroom

M: I follow giddy with excitement as I notice other men watching, they stare at my dress as it hangs open showing my erect nipples

D: you are not the only girl in there, my buddy and another are already doubling your girlfriend and I waste little time as I push you into a stall

M: mmmm…what do you want?

D: you prop your leg on the john as I unzip my pants exposing my hard erection to you

M: I reach down and feel it, stroking it like I've wanted to do since the first time I saw you, it makes me so wet I can almost feel myself dripping down my leg

D: I pull your dress up to your waist and then finger your pussy roughly

M: ahhhhhhhh I shudder, almost wanting to pull away, but, I need it so badly

D: damn baby your cunt is dripping wet I exclaim—you hear laughter from the adjoining stall

M: I can't help it. I'm so hot for you

D: I line my cock up and plunge hard into you

M: ahhhhh, oh my gawd I scream.. yess.. yesssss

D: feeling your pussy lubricate my cock I grab your hands and hold them tight over your head as we hump hard against each other like to animals

M: yes.. fuck me baby.. fuck me I scream, telling you I have to have all your cock as I rock my pelvis grinding into you, taking every inch of you

D: we fuck hard and savagely both racing towards a quick satisfying cum

M: yessss

D: looking up you see pervs leering at you over the stall wall

M: I can barely stay standing I'm getting so dizzy, I don't even realize they are watching

D: We hear your friend shouting at us to hurry up—obviously she is satiated

M: oh you feel so good

D: I pump you faster as I approach my orgasm

M: mmmm.. yeah baby, I begin to explode onto you, I cum so much that it puddles on the floor and you almost slip in it

D: I feel your cunt squeezing me as I cum inside you

M: the bystanders have never seen such an orgasm, I grab your ass and pull you into me, I feel your juices shoot into me hotly

D: I finish cumming inside of you and when I pull out our juices dribble down your leg as I catch my breath

M: my pussy throbs, I push back my long bangs now dripping with sweat and sticking to my face

D: I kiss you deeply and say, "Hi, I'm Dennis"

M: mmmmm..."Hi Dennis, I'm Marie, nice to fuck you"

D: laughing I look down at us and say—clean me up, my cock is coated with our lust

M: I sit obediently on the toilet, taking your cock in my mouth and sucking greedily I take it in until my lips are pressed against your balls

D: ahhh...easy, my cock is so sensitive after a cum

M: I suck deep and hard but then pull away

D: after I feel clean I grab my handkerchief and wet it then return it so you can clean yourself up a bit. Mmmm..."Marie, I need a little break but would love to bring you back to my place a little later for another round"

M: yes I would love that Dennis, I'm sure there are many other ways we could pleasure each other. I pull myself together as much as I can.

D: I reach in my jacket and pull out a very special bead and wrap it around your waist. "I'll go get us another round meet me outside when you are ready."

M: I kiss you deeply, sucking your bottom lip in, "In a few baby, I'll be there." I go with my friend to the ladies room. We are both flushed with excitement.

D: I grab us fresh hurricanes and wait outside chatting quickly with my buddies

M: I clean myself up as best I can but now I have no panties and my thigh highs are sticky with our sex

D: I have sucked down half a drink by the time you arrive

M: your buddies are almost blocking the doorway when I come. I make sure that I brush my nipples across the chest of one, as I squeeze through, than I walk to you and put my arms around you.

D: the five of us wander around the streets for the next hour partying and having a good time. We stop and do shooters than wander into an off beat bar

M: this is one of the most thrilling nights of my life, I look forward to each minute, wondering what we will do

D: this bar has girls dancing and stripping yet they aren't pros

M: I watch them and feel the need to join one of them. She is looking at you, I know she wants you

D: We encourage the two of you to get up and dance for the bar, smiling at you I kiss you deep then using my knife I cut the fabric of your dress so it is now a mini—this I hope makes you my total slut. The three of us guys sit back in the round corner booth as you and your friend leave us to dance.

M: We strut up and down the stage moving to the music. They have a pole to play with, and I begin to slide up and down on it, which is easy considering how wet I am

D: my friends and I fire up stogies congratulating ourselves on such good luck

M: I step backstage and gather up a few things to use for your show…a feather boa, gloves…a fan, I want you to enjoy this evening like nothing you have ever had before. I come back to your table and the slut that was watching you earlier has moved over to your table and is now trying to seduce you. I walk up and push her back a bit, but than I start to dance with her. She is startled but then excited, she tells me she loves my huge breasts. For a moment she forgets about you and dances for me. I pretend to be interested but then turn and wink at you

D: my friends and I line up some bills on the rail just for good measure

M: I don't want to share you. I want you for myself

D: we comment how sexy you both are and urge you two to inter-act for us

M: she wants to do whatever you want because she too wants you...I dance with her...watching your face, seeing you grinning, I lean over and kiss you again. She wants to do the same but I pull her back onto the stage and we dance closely together. She puts her hand on my breast...I let her

D: I smile back at you—my face filled with lust

M: she wants to touch me more, I can feel that, but I want you

D: I watch your gorgeous curves barely hidden by your now tat-tered dress

M: she tries to lick my nipples but I don't let her. She turns to you again and tries to dance just for you. I pull her back, pull her close, grab her hand...and she thinks I am going to kiss her. I take her hand and move it between my legs.

D: ohh damn that is hot

M: I push our fingers against my still steaming slit, as her fingers get soaked she gets more excited, then...

D: we cheer and urge you on

M: I pull her close and tell her, that's him on your fingers bitch and that's as close as you're ever gonna get! Then I push her back onto the stage and move back to you, giving you the most erotic lap dance you have ever seen

D: whistling and applauding I put down my cigar and kiss you

M: we kiss deeply and I say "Lets go baby, I want you to myself for awhile."

D: I say adios to my friends and walk away with you. We walk about a block and I hail a cab. Looking at you I tell you I'm sharing a flat with four roomies...your place?

M: I'm only here visiting but I do have a hotel room, with a whirlpool

D: you give the driver directions—it's about a 20 minute ride

M: I begin to kiss you again, I've never wanted anyone the way I desire you

D: we kiss and my fingers trace your inner thighs making you hot

M: I put my hands up under you shirt so I can feel your chest, then I unbutton your pants and pull them down a bit...I kiss your stomach
D: mmmmm...wait for the whirlpool hun...besides, I kiss your neck and ear
M: ohh yesss
D: and whisper...flash the driver baby, show him that sweet pussy I am going to be fucking. I nibble on your ear and neck making you hotter
M: I lay one leg over you, our bodies close, you're still nibbling on me as I put my other leg up against the seat on my side. I run my hand down my thigh and finger myself
D: I whisper...you're so sexy. The driver watches.
M: I take your hand in mine
D: let me taste you
M: mmmm.. oh yes baby please do
D: I suck on your finger
M: we almost fly forward as the cab screeches to a stop...the driver almost rear ending someone while watching us
D: giggling we pay our fare as we leave the cab and run up to your room
M: I pull you into the elevator and kiss you madly again. I want you so.
D: my finger slides along your slit, teasing your clit
M: I'm so hot I'm dripping...I can't wait to feel the heat of your cock pounding into me again. The elevator opens, we get to my door and I can barely unlock it. We go in and I take off your jacket and shirt. I bite your nipples lightly, I pull away to go start the water in the tub.
D: I walk over and ask you what would you like to drink?
M: call room service, order whatever you like and strawberries and whip cream, lots and lots of whipped cream...oh and see if they have any chocolate syrup ok? ☺
D: laughing I place the order along with a bottle of champagne and bourbon
M: while leaning over into the tub to fumble with the stopper, I hear you come up behind me.
D: they said about ten minutes...oh my, noticing your fine ass up in the air I kiss it and tease you saying while I wait for room service why don't you fix up your makeup and start in the tub.
M: I laugh and give you a peck and say ok. Checking myself in the mirror for the first time since the bar I notice that I'm a complete mess!

I clean myself up smiling the whole time at the incredible good luck of running into you. I take off what I was wearing and after some quick cleansing with the washcloth I slip into the little black satin nightie I had brought along.

D: Prepping the room service I put everything on a table near the whirlpool. Then I freshen my drink and pour you some champagne. I also lay the roses I had them bring for you around its edge. I whistle as you walk in the room.

M: oh baby, thank you so much, I take the drink but kiss you first, then sip at it teasingly. Are you ready for the tub?

D: sure baby. I put down my drink and start to take off my shirt...shoes...and socks.

M: I watch...eagerly

D: I then pull down my jeans...slowly

M: I really haven't seen you, we were so close in the stall...

D: I stretch and then take my boxers down and turn around so you can check me out

M: woohoooooooo I hoot

D: you like? I smirk

M: oh yes baby I do, I do. I walk up to you and put my arms over your shoulders and my nightie lightly brushes against your cock, I kiss you again

D: mmmmmm...the satin feels so cool, I kiss you back slowly

M: I whisper in your ear...slip it off me, lets go to the tub

D: I'm better with my knife I joke as I slowly pull it off revealing your breasts, and than the rest of you

M: I giggle...mmmmm...I move close enough to have my nipples brush against yours then I take your hand and walk toward the tub

D: ahh the water feels so good

M: I step in front of you and I sit with my back on the tub, I motion for you to sit in front of me, your back to my front. I grab a washcloth and begin to massage your back with it, rubbing you all over.

D: ohhh I groan

M: sudsing you up

D: mmmm you read my mind

M: working my fingers I massage you loosening up all the tight muscles

D: I relax and sip my drink

M: I grab the oil that I left by the side of the tub and work it into your neck, over your shoulders...down your arms...you lean back so my breasts cushion you

D: mmmmmmmmmmmmmmmmm

M: I reach around you, massaging your face...than your chest. You are totally relaxed. I take a strawberry from the bowl and feed it to you

D: I eat it slowly, watching you, enjoying being pampered by you

M: mmmmm I smile and pull you close

D: I wrap my arms in yours and kiss them

M: I ask you softly, "Would you like to sit on the edge of the tub and let me finish what I started in the cab?

D: water splashes over the edge of the tub as I hurry to my perch. You move over to me still in the water, steam making your face glisten I take my hand and brush some of the hair from your face so I can look into your eyes

M: moving close to you I smile and put my hands on your hips

D: I kiss you deeply first—this has been a great evening

M: I move back down to your knees and kiss my way up the insides of each thigh

D: my cock throbs

M: I love seeing how hard you are for me. I grab the whipped cream and fill my mouth with it, then I put your cock in with it, the cream surrounds you while I suck

D: mmmmm.. very nice baby, but now its time for me to go

M: aawwwwww

D: thanks, I would like to pick this up again

M: I would too

D: bye for now

M: you like?

D: yup, ran through a few dif fantasies ☺

M: mmmmmmmmmmmmmmmmmmmmmmmmmmmmm

D: I'm glad you did too, too bad your panties are on the wall ;)

M: LOL...thanks baby

D: see you later

M: bye

The woman's role throughout life is a passive and the man's an active one. And in choosing a mate the man will always be the active factor or pursuer. So biology seems to tell us. Whether education-using the word in its broadest sense-will effect a radical change in the relation of man and woman remains to be seen. A change putting the man and the woman on a footing of equality would be desirable; but whether biological differences having their roots in the remotest antiquity can be obliterated, is a question the answer of which lies in the distant future.

Woman: Her Sex and Love Life

Hot Luvin'

Tiring of meeting men that lived far, far away I placed an ad on a more local singles sight. I received a lot of response but mostly from incompatible old men or boys. Until this one:

Hey there Miss Marie,
I have checked out your ad and profile. I thought they looked pretty interesting, and I liked what you had written. I'd like to know more. Well anyway, hope you had a good weekend, and hope to hear from you again.
Will

I went and checked out his profile.

Location: 30 miles from me, Age: 31, Athletic/Fit, 6ft 1inch, Non-smoker, Occasional Drinker, No children.
Add Title: Nice guy seeks "girl next door"
Hello out there! If you are like me, you have found that finding your perfect match is about impossible. I am 31, in shape, good job and I feel I have a good sense of humor, am compassionate, and a good listener who is very open minded and laid back. The perfect woman for me (but I'm not looking for perfection, just highly compatible) would be funny, have a good self-image, values honesty

and trust. A woman that has a career and is as driven as I am to get the most out of life. I am looking for a woman that is not afraid to go after what she wants, and preferably close in location. I am not looking for a long distance relationship. Been there did that, didn't work! Also because of business reasons, relocation for me is not possible. I am 31 years old and want to have children by the time I am 35. I want to be able to grow up with my children, and not look like their grandpa at graduation!! I love the out-doors, sports, playing volleyball, people watching, and stimulating conversation. If you are looking for a person that will be totally honest and straight forward drop me a line. Hope to hear from you. Will

I liked what I read, wrote him back and then connected online via messenger service.

Will: so what possessed you to put out a personals ad?
Marie: no single people around here
Will: yeah I hear that, or at least single people that one would want to spend any amount of time with
Marie: right, locals that are single...I know why, and I don't want them either!
Will: had any good response to your ad??
Marie: about 60 in the last week
Will: WOW, that is a lot, way more than mine, but I do think women get a better response rate than men. Meet any yet?
Marie: one
Will: how was it?
Marie: nice guy
Will: uh oh, the "nice guy" curse, for him anyway
Marie: lol, I don't know, just not the sparks I was hoping for
Will: so what caught your eye about my ad?
Marie: sounded honest
Will: it was, that is the way I am, I will be honest, even if I know some toes will get stepped on
Marie: that is what I'm looking for
Will: me too, the last woman I was seriously involved with was a compulsive liar. I'm not sure she even knew what honesty was.
Marie: I hate that, or...someone that won't say what's really on their mind, or someone with very little mind.

Will: I think she believed the lies and stories she told. I found out way to late, she was really good at it. That's a good way to put it...little mind, or conscience.

Marie: Yes

Will: I would rather hear something "bad" now than down the road when it is too late, or the damage that has been done is irreversible.

Marie: Right. Hmmm...sorry I'm so tired, I'm kind of dragging

Will: do not take this the wrong way, but I have met many women that say these things, but do not really believe them. Sorry about the skepticism.

Marie: it's okay I understand. I've been played by people on here, I'm not looking for that, I hope to find someone for forever

Will: I am looking for someone real and honest with themselves and with the world. I would love to find someone forever, thought I had that twice, but was wrong

Marie: I thought so once, but I was wrong too

Will: tough lesson to learn

Marie: I feel like I wasted 16yrs

Will: I feel I wasted 12, but at least you have a daughter to show for it.

Marie: I know, but she came before we were married, I should have just taken her and left him be.

Will: but that would not have been the "right" thing to do, being a single mom was not a "good" thing, if you get my meaning

Marie: I know, but I was damned determined to make it work...to prove everyone wrong, etc.

Will: I have several female friends that are single mothers, there are very few people that I have more respect for than my single mother friends, it takes a strong woman to make it work.

Marie: yes it does

Will: do you feel you have been a success at single motherhood?

Marie: VERY!

Will: good for you that is wonderful!

Marie: she is beautiful, brilliant, self sufficient, funny...etc!!

Will: do you see a lot of yourself in her? Both the good and the bad?

Marie: mostly the good, she is me now...not the me I was when I was her age

Will: what's different?

Marie: I was a follower, not a leader and I didn't stand up for myself. I had very little self-confidence

Will: she is more driven and independent than you were at her age?

Marie: yes, I've made her that way since she was little

Will: you and her get along well I take it

Marie: she takes care of me...lol

Will: does she know of your internet search for Mr. Right?

Marie: god yes, I share everything with her, too much so I'm sure, but, I don't hide much

Will: what does she think of this meeting guys on the computer?

Marie: she is hoping I find someone great

Will: does she meet the guys you date?

Marie: She did meet the last one

Will: do they have to meet her approval? LOL

Marie: yes I think so, but she's me...so if I like, she would too

Will: so a guy has to pass the test of 2 women!?

Marie: yup, are you up for it?

Will: I will try anything once, twice if I like it! Well, almost anything!

Marie: woohooo...twice?? Like...in the same night?? Hehehe

Will: if you are up for it! Actually I prefer to wait a bit for that sort of thing, I talk big, and joke about sex a lot, but that is a very important and special thing.

Marie: agreed, but it is important

Will: I just don't go there with anybody. Sex important??

Marie: yes, you have to be compatible. If you don't have similar drives someone will feel left out

Will: exactly, compatible emotionally, psychologically and physically

Marie: right! That is what I hope to find!

Will: there has to be an attraction on a lot of different levels, you may find someone stimulating in their conversations, but not at all physically, or the other way around, it is hard to find someone that can fulfill all or at least most of your needs.

Marie: I had a man online that wrote me amazing letters, great conversations, etc. but he wasn't all the way off the plane and I knew there were no sparks.

Will: that's happened with me too, well with women I mean! LOL

Marie: I felt sooo guilty, he had the bridal suite and I left him standing there almost crying.

Will: sheeeeesh, think he expected a little too much for the first in person meeting?

Marie: oh it wasn't supposed to be the bridal suite they gave him an upgrade, but still it was way to much and he didn't expect the sex but I think was ready just in case.
Will: most guys are hoping for sex, then see what else happens
Marie: but, what do you really think if you get it the first meeting?
Will: like I said, sex for me anyway, comes after I get to know a woman, and feel really comfortable with her, I think that sex on the first meeting can really confuse the relationship.
Marie: true
Will: I mean is the relationship going to be built on sex, or friendship and trust
Marie: I'd like it on all three
Will: me too, all three and of course other factors are very important, you have to have the right balance.

This was really fun for me. An interesting, intelligent man not afraid to lay it all out on the table. We met at his house and went out for dinner that Saturday. He was polite and quiet. We ate and talked and than played a few games of pool. He didn't stare at my chest or brush up against me or give me any indication of whether or not he was still interested in me. I hated that. I always think the worst, but I guess the worst would have been him pretending to go to the bathroom and ditching me at some point in the evening…whew, that didn't happen. We went back to his house and he had a few more beers while we watched a movie together.

I don't remember the exact details…something about back-aches and massages and before he knew it we were kissing and I got him to agree to go to his room. I just hate a man that puts out on the first date…not. Okay, I admit that having sex makes me feel like I'm wanted. I like the rush of the unknown, and at that moment the hairiest man I'd ever seen was coming towards me. In the darkness he looked a little like a furry rug that had the fibers rubbed off of it in one spot…that spot on him surrounded his genitals…and there was something else different, the glint from a piece of jewelry right on his shaft. I was fascinated. Apparently shaving his package was a daily ritual and he did a fine job. The jewelry didn't seem to have any noticeable effect during the love-making (yes I said the ☹ word, even though I ummm…sorta seduced him it wasn't really just fucking) but I liked the thought of it.

We cuddled and I spent the night. It was very nice and I actually left hoping I'd see him again soon. He left me some sweet offline messages and we chatted often. It was kind of strange being so honest with each other. We admitted that since our personal ads were new there were other people we wanted to meet.

We agreed to go ahead and have other dates and we always discussed them with each other. Than we agreed we both needed a little physical attention and he invited me over for dinner.

I dressed up for him and by the time I got to his house he already had his grill going. He gave me a drink and had me sit down to visit him while he prepared the rest of our meal. A man that can cook definitely has my attention. He fussed about chopping all kinds of things for his famous home-made salsa and the pork chops had been marinating for hours, it all smelled wonderful. We ate and watched a movie together, or maybe just part of a movie…LOL, it didn't take us long to get naked and in bed together. He was a great kisser and I was really warming up to him, but wait…I was getting warmer, and warmer…and all of a sudden…burning…ooowww…ouchieeee…omg…"What are you doing with your fingers??" Okay, my pussy is now aching and not in the pleasant way! I push him off me and let him know something is not right. He takes his fingers out of me. "What the hell, did you not wash your hands after cutting those peppers?"

Will stands up by the side of the bed bewildered. He watches me squirm for a bit and then gets a case of the giggles…he than goes to wipe a tear from his eye and manages to put some of the hot pepper residue into his eye. Now he starts jumping around saying it burns and I get the giggles between my own burning spasms! He runs to the bathroom and starts to try and flush his eye out with water. Than he comes back and asks me what he can do to help. I suggest, err demand, that he plant his face between my thighs and keeps on licking until I feel better. Eventually things cooled down.

We stayed friends online and off but never tried the sex thing again. I really liked his next girlfriend and I was even invited to their wedding.

Infatuation and Being in Love. While, as said, the feeling of love does not readily lend itself to dissection, to analysis, still we can differentiate some phases of it. We can differentiate between "being in love," "infatuation," and "love." Being in love is, as just indicated, a pathological, morbid phenomenon. The person who is in love is not in a normal condition. He can see nothing, he cannot be argued with, as far as his love is concerned.

Woman: Her Sex and Love Life

Reflection of My Affection

I have a hard time trying to figure out why some people come into your life and others don't. On the rare occasions that I feel that gut pulling, heart stopping sense I have to meet someone, I like to take it. When I loved my ex I had a strong connection to him. Even though he traveled with work back and forth across the country…I always knew approximately where he was. I could also "feel" when he was getting close to home. I lost that sense when I stopped caring about him…or…maybe I blocked that sense because he started cheating on me.

Even though this one still hurts, I want to share it with you. I met David in a dating chat service. His profile caught my eye right away: 6'2, brown hair, blue eyes, goatee, single, average looking (I don't care for the men that think they're gorgeous even if they are), and it said he worked construction (LOVE a man that is good with his hands). His extended profile stated that he was: very passionate and supportive, extremely loving and sincere, romantic, warm, totally faithful with a good sense of humor. To top it off under the goal of belonging to this service he had checked, romance/relationship.

I messaged him and he was all I'd hoped and more. He was silly and kind. He could take a joke and give a joke. He loved animals and spoke of his dog often. Exotic woods were his passion and his dream was to one day have his own shop where he'd make custom furniture pieces. I was giddy from the excitement of finding him. I happily bounced around doing my work and chores all day knowing that I could chat with him again in the evenings.

After a few nights of chatting we decided to move to the level of phone conversation. I loved talking on the phone but was nervous about hearing his voice. You know I have that stupid thing in my head that I think I will know the right man by his voice…<sigh>. When he did finally call me, he was a nervous as I was, but the voice melted me. It fit perfectly in with the rest of him. We laughed…we talked…we had deep conversations about our dreams and our heartaches. I longed to be close to him. We hated having to hang up with each other. I was content to just hold the phone tight and hear him breath. I wanted to curl up with him and fall asleep listening to the beating of his heart.

I wrote him email when I got online before he did. This was the first one:

Subject: Who are you?
Who are you…
To come into my life
So suddenly.
Who are you…
To push out others that
Had my attention
And make me forget about them.
Who are you…
To put a smile on my face
Anytime you cross my mind.
Who are you…
To make me want to believe
That there really is someone out there
That wants to be loved like I do.
Who are you?
And when can I look into your eyes
And wrap my arms around you
And make sure you're real.
Xoxoxoxoxox, Marie

I had so fallen for this man. I meant every word I chatted and wrote to him. There were no games…no saying things just to get his reaction. No chatting with ten other men behind his back. He had my full attention and I was so happy. That was before I got this email in return to mine:

Subject: I am yours!
Marie,
I didn't come into your life. I was brought into your life.
I didn't push the others away, I just pulled you closer.
The smile on your face is simply a reflection of my affection for you,
And just so you know…
There is someone out here that wants to hold you as much if not more

Than you want to hold them.
I'm sure you'll have my soul at that very instant.
I've met a lot of women but no one as beautiful inside
And out as you.
You have my heart,
My soul,
My attention,
My being.
I hope you don't throw it away.
Love, David

OMG!!! Can you believe that response! Like I wasn't already crazy for this man. All the kindness, love and romance missing in my life was right there in Denver. I hurried to write back something I hoped would be worthy of his affections.

Subject: Re: I am yours!
Dearest David,
I'm still basking in the warmth of your kind words.
The walls surrounding my heart have crumbled into a
Footpath to my soul that beckons you to walk it.
I can't allow myself fear or questioning...when they try
To surface all the good thoughts of you just wash
The worry away and leave me with a sense of peace
That I have never felt before. I long to hold you in
My arms, and be held by yours...the distance has its
Disadvantages but yet is meaningless as long as
I have you in my heart...and right now, my heart
Already feels more whole than ever before.
Okay...I'm making myself tear up...;-)
Just know I'm thinking of you constantly,
Yours, Marie

There, I had done it. Put my fragile little heart right out there in the open. I was happy to do it. Our online and phone conversations continued. I went to mapquest and found out he was eight hundred miles from me. Since he was busy with work and I could get away I suggested that I come to see him. He said he didn't want me to do that but would rather wait a couple weeks and try to drive to me. I'm not a very patient person when it comes to matters of the heart but I agreed. Secretly I still hoped to just hop in my truck and surprise him.

Our feeling for each other scared us. I tried to leave myself open to the possibility of love…but I could feel him putting some walls up. We talked about his fears. I was terrified he was going to shut me out. A few uncomfortable conversations later I had mail.

Subject: none
Marie,
I'm sorry about last night and all the other nights. I guess I'm just not ready for this yet. You make me feel like I'm falling in love and that really scares me. I haven't had much luck in that dept. as of yet. And here I am contemplating picking up and moving to Minnesota just so I can try to make you fall in love with me. How crazy is that? I've got a career here that I really enjoy, yet I sometimes wonder if it's enough to make me happy. For the last five years or so I have been searching for the love of my life and because of that I always seem to rush into a relationship blinded by love or what I thought was love. So far it has ended up always being what I thought was love, so as soon as I make the mistake it's too late to turn back. I know if I come see you or visa versa right now, I will fall madly in love with you and leave everything I have established here. I know you're saying, "I never said to just pick up and move", but I know me, and when love takes over I have no control. I'd do it even if you told me not to. Even if you told me you didn't want a relationship with me, I'd still move so that I could try to persuade you into falling for me as I have for you. So I think the reason for my being a jerk is a defense mechanism that my heart has installed to protect me from being hurt. I really don't want to treat you bad, yet for some reason I do. I think I need some time to think about all this. I'll probably regret it. I'm not going to ask you to wait for me to figure this all out. That wouldn't be fair. I will tell you that you will hear from me again, and my feelings for you haven't changed. I just need some time to figure out how to stop being afraid of my heart. I am so sorry for the way I've been acting. You don't deserve that at all. I hope you don't put me in the same class as "the assholes". I'm not saying I don't want this. I just need to get my shit together.
Sincerely, David
p.s. I have never met anyone who has unlocked my heart as fast as you. I'll call you in a few days. Please don't hate me.

I fell from my cloud in the sky and hit the ground so hard it knocked all the wind right out of me. I couldn't breath. I called his number. He didn't answer. I had such a terrible sense of loss. Part of me was missing. I ached. I emailed him back, tried not to be too needy, but begged him to let me into his heart. I wept.

Days and days of no contact with David made me a mess. My work suffered, my body suffered…and I'm sure my daughter suffered too. She knew how much I had cared about this stranger in Colorado. We'd discussed possibly moving there. I was going to have the man of my dreams and she would have the mountains.

When I finally did have some contact with David through chat it was obvious things had changed. He had shut himself off and I wasn't going to be allowed the access I used to have. It hurt so much to let go of him, but I did. I imagine I probably got angry and emailed him something kind of nasty but I don't remember that. All I remember is how much I cared.

After a couple weeks of mourning I went back to the dating service and continued my search. I gathered up most of the stones from that path to my heart and built a new barricade…thicker and stronger than the last. I would be more careful. I wouldn't fall so fast. That was my new plan.

Six months later I got a phone call. It was David. He was in tears as he told me how sorry he was for shutting me out and how he had missed me so. I put timbers up to brace the barricade but they didn't hold. I broke down and through my own tears told how the only thing that mattered was now…I couldn't be mad at him. I just hoped he was okay. We talked for the next few days. It was almost like before. I told him I wasn't going to let him run from me again. I booked a flight to go see him.

Two days later I was in Colorado. I called David and told him I was there. He asked, "Where?"

"Here in Denver!!" I cheerfully replied.

"Oh, I didn't think you were serious," was his response.

The tone of his voice had changed. I got a terrible feeling. I knew he was at work and that it was a surprise to him so I tried not to over think his response. I tried not to sound worried. I let him know that I was picking up a rental car and going to find a hotel fairly close to where he lived. He said he'd call me after work. I got the car and drove around the city for a couple hours. I settled into a reasonably cheap and crappy hotel and waited for his call. I waited…waited…and waited. I started calling his cell and home numbers. He wouldn't answer. He never answered. He never called. I was a pathetic loser eight hundred miles from home…I was so alone.

I tried to tell myself there was a reason I was there. I searched and searched for that silver lining on my cloud of unhappiness. I spent a day at the zoo. Being near animals has always been my greatest source of comfort. Animals don't lie to you. Animals seek out kindness. Animals have always been my truest friends.

I drove around aimlessly. Well almost aimlessly…I knew I was within a couple blocks of his home. I just couldn't bring myself to get any closer. He hadn't called…I wasn't wanted. I wouldn't push anymore. Rocky Mountain National Park was beautiful. I took a lot of pictures. Hard to focus through the blur of tears…hard to be happy when you're so sad. Hard to keep going…but I did.

Premature baldness is a decidedly inheritable trait. And so is premature grayness of the hair. But it is doubtful if any woman would permit these factors to play any role in her choice of a husband.

Woman: Her Sex and Love Life

Smells Like...

I thought I'd try hooking up with another somewhat local man. He had a nice profile and a very nice picture. Sparkling dark eyes and a killer smile complete with dimples. YUM! He was divorced and my height. He was wearing a cowboy hat in his photo, which isn't really my thing but he looked like a real stallion in it. Later on I learned through our conversations that the poor thing had beautiful long curly locks that started just above the edge of that hat, and no hair on the top. Damn.

He wanted to meet me, but preferred to wait until after his appointment at some hair farm up in the cities. After he'd been there he came to my home and we went for a walk around the farm. I didn't completely understand what procedure he'd had but he was now sporting a full head of hair that looked quite natural.

We went in to watch a movie and made out on my couch. He told me he hadn't had sex with anyone since his wife and him split over a year before. I fucked him on my floor. Apparently I've become some kind of divorce land welcome wagon. His head smelled like adhesive...I didn't see him again...guess he didn't want our relationship to get...sticky.

That's all I have to say about that.

Just as we have impotent and excessively libidinous men, so we have frigid and excessively libidinous women. A wife possessed of excessive libido is a terrible calamity for a husband of a normal or moderate sexuality. Many a libidinous wife has driven her husband, especially if she is young and he is old, to a premature grave. And "grave" is used in the literal, not figurative, sense of the word. It would be a good thing if a man could find out the character of his future wife's libido before marriage. Unfortunately, it is impossible. At best, it can only be guessed at. But a really excessive libido on the part of either husband or wife should constitute a valid ground for divorce.

Woman: Her Sex and Love Life

Mc...Who?

Occasionally I meet someone in chat that doesn't live too far away from me. Since I'm in the sticks, it means someone within fifty miles is practically next door, woohoo! I think the first time I chatted Ron it was really late and he was working and I should have been sleeping. He said he was a Registered Nurse and I shouldn't make fun of him but I thought it was great since my mom had been a nurse too. We gave each other a hard time teasing about things and flirting and it was fun.

Ron was thirty-four and just and inch shorter me, but I thought I could get over my height issues. The real red flag popped up when he admitted his divorce wasn't final yet. He assured me he had been moved out of the house for a year and that their situation just wasn't going to work out. I put up a bit of a wall against him and decided to just keep him a chat friend. I told him about Amber and how strange it was having an almost grown daughter and he told me about Mark-2 and Kelly-4. I couldn't believe that someone could move out on his wife when their babies were so young but on the other hand I do feel that if you aren't getting along it is better to be apart and happy than together and miserable.

We continued to chat whenever we were both online. I told him about other men I was interested in and he let me know how hard it was juggling two jobs and trying to spend as much time as possible with his kids. I found myself thinking how nice it would be to have two more kids that I didn't have to gain a ton of weight for…and Ron kept telling me how nice it would be to live on a farm.

I'm going to let the rest of this story play out by sharing with you some of the offline messages, chat conversations, and emails I saved. Keep in mind that there were many more and besides all of the internet contacts we eventually called each other two or three times a day.

∗   ∗   ∗   ∗   ∗

The following are messages left for me through an Internet messenger service. It's always a thrill for me to log on and have offline messages pop up. I love feeling that someone is thinking about me and maybe even missing me when I'm not there. These are just a few samples of messages left for me over a one month period when this Medic guy was becoming a friend.

Medic: so you still around? what is the story? you and this guy an item now? has he came to his senses on horse poop? get back to me and let me know what time you will be on.
Medic: I am right here! call me sometime or tell me what time you are on the here thang! 507-555-0482
Medic: hey silly kid! so when can i bring the tikes over to see the horses? how are ya? haven't heard from ya lately. Ron
Medic: ok so what about that lunch date?
Medic: are you going to be around on Friday? I will have the kids I guess/but that is the next time that I will have work off for a awhile
Medic: Hey sorry I missed you yesterday/it would have been fun to have done something/I didn't get any messages from you about doing anything so I just packed it for up north. lets do breakfast this week, how does that sound? I work tonight and all week/but I have my days open.
Medic: you still on?
Medic: hey you!
Medic: let me know if a day will work this week that we can do lunch or something?
Medic: did I tell you that I make horse leads—what size do you like best?
Medic: hey I just got back and don't remember what I wrote, I am at work/I think that my little guy has a Doc appt. at around lunch

time on Wed. if that is the case I can sure come over after that anyways I will check it out and call ya or send you another email tomorrow/I have all day Thursday open/I am waiting on a rope shipment that should take another 3-4 weeks and then you can take your pick, I will have tons of 10". talk to you later
Medic: that appointment that I have on Wednesday is at 3:30 so I could do something at or before lunch time. Or let me know if Thursday works ok, later
Medic: I will let you sleep I wish I was! I will call you in the morning at around 7ish if you are up b-4 that call my cell
Medic: I can get a nap and be over sometime around 11? and we can do lunch or whatever you like, it is completely up to you

I agreed to let Ron come see me for a lunch date. He came to my house and we worked a couple hours fixing horse fences and just talking. It was so sweet having someone help me out! I started thinking I should have let him come see me weeks ago! We continued online conversations whenever he had a spare moment at work and I happened to be online, if I didn't connect he would leave me more offline messages.

Medic: Hey, Thanks for having me over I had a lot of fun. You have an awesome place I don't think its a good idea for me to bringing my kids over cuz I will never be able to get them to leave! Call me when you whenever you like. Talk to you later sexy!
Medic: get up and talk to me!
Medic: stop staying out all night and you won't have to sleep all day
Medic: I had a big bloody welt on my leg right below my ass where your horse bit me! I should come show ya

(Fri 11/02, 11:40 AM)
He came back to my house. We hugged and kissed and couldn't keep our hands off each other. We got naked. It was goooooooooooood. I prefer sex with candles and some fat disguising darkness but it is great when it is the middle of the day and you just can't wait. He seemed to fit into my home, my life, my body…perfectly.

Medic: So tell me about the weekend? mmmm male stripers? gangbangs? all one big drunkin' party, well you can invite me you know!

Medic: hey what are you doing on Thursday I have the day with the kids, and what are you doing every day for that matter?
Medic: well I have nuttin' goin on Thursday yet so...I will call ya later on today or tomorrow k?
Medic: wow nice new pic on your profile? What's up

(Fri 11/09, 11:30 AM)

In between all of our offline messages and online chats we talked on the phone whenever Ron would have a few minutes. He'd offer to come and help with my horse or yard projects and let me know that in the future when we were together things would be easier. He was bringing his kids over with him for lunch and I was so nervous about meeting them. I cooked a roast for Ron and made the back up of macaroni and cheese with hotdogs for the kids. Ron was carrying little Marky when they got to my door. His pretty blonde hair was all tousled like he'd been sleeping in the car and I knew right away he wasn't thrilled to be here, not yet anyway. Luckily Kelly was all smiles as she came to meet me, well...me or my house cat Kenny but either way she was happy.

We sat down to eat and Mark fussed. Ron seemed quite irritated that he wasn't behaving better. I reminded him the boy was just two and that he shouldn't worry. The macaroni and cheese was definitely a good idea but I forgot what tiny servings two and four year olds eat. Kelly visited while she ate and I found her adorable. After lunch Ron was holding Mark and I asked Kelly if she'd like to go out and feed the horses with me. She was so cute stomping around in a pair of old boots I'd found for her to wear and she was a real trooper trying to help with whatever she could. The animals all seemed to enjoy her as much as I was.

I got Sandy, my oldest mare, out of the pasture and put a child's sized saddle on her. Kelly brushed her and fed her some treats. She let me pick her up and put her in the saddle, than she smiled so big it almost looked like it hurt. I walked Sandy up to the house and Ron and Mark came out to join us. We put Mark behind Kelly and he actually smiled. Sandy was careful to take small slow steps as to not scare her precious cargo. I handed Ron the rope and ran to get my camera. I got some great pictures of my three new ranch hands. When it was time to put Sandy away Mark was okay with it and Kelly was sad but I like that. I need more kids that can't get enough of the horses.

We came back in and I put a movie in for the kids. Kelly came right over and crawled up on my lap. Ron scolded her for being so forward and she put her arms around me and told her dad that she liked me better than him. I let him know I didn't mind and inside I was so damn happy that I had the Kelly stamp of approval. Mark's eyes started looking a little watery and Ron said he needed to take him home for some children's medicine.

I wished they could stay longer but at the same time I didn't want to risk having things turn bad on me. I got a quick hug from Ron and away they went.

Medic (Fri 11/09, 06:56 PM) Hi, Just wanted to say thanks for having us over today it was a lot of fun and thanks again for lunch. The kids had a blast. I have no idea why they were so terrible today (even worse than the normal terrible) I think that Mark was not feeling well and they were both very tired.
Medic (Fri 11/09, 07:00 PM) Well I have tried two babysitters for tomorrow night and no luck yet. I will call you tomorrow, okay? If it does not work out to see you tomorrow what is your schedule for next week? I would like to see you again sometime soon, and I don't care what we do I could always just buzz over some night for a movie or something. I have a couple days off next week but then work the weekend again, bye

(Chat 11/10, 09:39 AM)
Marie: hi...
Medic: What's up?
Marie: waiting...waiting
Medic: well what I said was that I have never had any trouble finding someone to baby-sit before and that I don't really get to see them all that much so I don't mind staying at home with them.
Marie: I don't blame you
Medic: I just wish that we had gone to the cities so my mom could have watched them, she begs to watch because she is like two hours away
Marie: your kids were great, Mark was just tired and getting sick
Medic: I also said that I would make it up to you
Marie: I know, I'm making a list
Medic: OUCH, but...I bet it would be fun!
Marie: Yes there may be some pain involved!
Medic: lead me to your shackles
Marie: uh huh, I don't think that you even like me, you're blowing me off aren't you
Medic: What!? You don't think that do you?
Marie: I never know what to think, so I try not too

Medic: well I think that you are awesome. I just don't know what to think about your man situation you know?

Marie: the situation is that I blew off all of them for you, and now here I sit

Medic: phone, just a second

Marie: I would like more than just someone to play with once in awhile

Medic: mmmmm me too. BRB its my mom on the phone

Marie: no problem, I'm editing the other pics I took of you and the kids

Medic: that is really cool the kids look great, thank you!

*   *   *   *   *

(Chat 11/17, 12:14 AM)

Medic: Still up?

Marie: hi! I was just going to head up to bed, was wondering what you were up too, I've been filling in all my online buds about you. ☺

Medic: oh really?

Marie: yes, NY is jealous but CA is happy for me

Medic: I get to sit all night and flirt with the big nurses

Marie: aww that's what you do??? Now I will find out you like me cause you're a chubby chaser??? LOL

Medic: last night I just sat and thought about you...chubby chaser?? Haha not in the least

Marie: anyone at work notice that your mind was elsewhere?

Medic: EVERYONE!

Marie: cool

Medic: I didn't have to say a word

Marie: I hope you are half as excited as I am

Medic: I was going to call you but I have to go do stuff every couple minutes

Marie: I understand

Medic: so what did you tell your friends about me? Did you tell them I was a lil shorty!

Marie: are you kidding! I said, xmas came early at my house.. woohoooo I finally got the big package!

Medic: sure you did, uRfunnygal—work calls I have to run again

Marie: okay ☹

Medic: I will not feel right calling you if you're sleeping but I do want to talk to you soon

Marie: leave me hot offline messages, I hope we can see each other again soon
Medic: me too, I can't wait
Marie: ty baby
Medic: bye
Marie: bye
Medic: uarethesexiestpersonontheplanet
Marie: awwwww…uareadorable & iwantmoreofu

From: Medic, To: Marie
Subject: Hey, Date: Saturday 17, Nov.
So are you getting these emails? Nice to see you on tonight and chat. It finally slowed down here so I could talk but it's 2:15am and I don't want to wake you if you're sleeping, so I won't call you. I don't even know if I made any sense tonight I had so much going on when I was chatting with you. At one point I was on the phone, talking to someone next to me, and chatting with you all at the same time (now that takes talent)
Well I don't know what is up for the weekend yet. I have to work that is for sure and I will call ya. Tomorrow night I work a different floor so it will be much slower and I can talk on the phone for a bit. Mmmmmmmmmmmmm guess what I am thinking about right now! LOL byes

From: Marie, To: Medic
Subject: hot stuff, Date: Saturday 17, Nov
Hi Hotstuff
Just thought I'd sneak online quick and leave you a couple pics so you don't forget about me!! I'm off to the FFA banquet for my kid, she is up for member of the year and some other awards!!! YEAH for the super kid! Anyway…I'll keep my cell with me and I hope to hear from you sometime tonight. Take care, Marie

From: Medic, To: Marie
Subject: Re: hot stuff, Date: Sun, 18th Nov 1am
OMG!
Thanks for the pics, WOW!!! You are miss dominatrix I like it! So if I come over this morning you will put that on for me? Mmmmuuuaaahaaawww

*Well I don't think that I will make it over today I am going to take
the kids to church and sleep. I will see you on Monday morning if
that works for you? I will call you later today, okay. Hope you had a
good night and are okay (being good and safe)*
BYE

From: Medic, To: Marie
Subject: sad, Date: Sun, 18 Nov 23:53
*Sorry I missed your call! I wanted to talk to you. It's too late to try
you now. We were busy in the ER tonight and still are. I'm still planning on seeing you in the morning. (even though the ducks are flying) talk to you later*

From: Medic, To: Marie
Date: November 20, 11am
*It was great seeing you yesterday. Sorry I forgot to take the hat
you gave me with me ☹ I loved the pic you sent me, you made that
hat look soooooooooo good! I will call you tonight. I just got up and I
have a couple of appointments this afternoon.*

From: Medic, To: Marie
Subject: Bath Time! Date: November 21, 6pm
*Very nice! I would love to take a bath with you! Well I am at Matt's
house because he is sick today and I will be staying home with
him, I will call you in a couple minutes and let you know that I will
not be right over to jump in bed with you ☹ That is what I was planning on doing! Maybe we can both stop over later if he is feeling
okay. Can we bring lunch??*

(Fri 11/23, 08:25 AM)
Medic: hey sweetie how was your turkey day? Hope you had fun, I
will call you later today and maybe even see you this weekend.
Would it be okay if I bring the kids over for a couple hours? I will
have them until Sunday afternoon.

(Chat Fri 11/23, 09:14 AM)
Medic: hey sweetie, who ya chatting with?
Marie: I just came online to look for messages from you! How was
your Thanksgiving?

Medic: do you know how much I miss you? I thought you looked great the other day

Marie: lol...you are a silly man

Medic: I was the one that looked bad

Marie: must be why I like you soooooooooooooooo much

Medic: I have to run, I will call you later today, okay?

Marie: You better! Take care...stay safe

Medic: u2 byeeeee, and change that profile! No chatting with the losers!!

Marie: I won't sweetie, I'm not looking anymore <wink>

Medic: cya, call ya later

Marie: bye

(Chat 11/27)

Marie: Do I know you?

Medic: Indeed you do!! What's up?

Marie: Ben tells me he shaves his balls...<wink> but I was looking for you

Medic: so who is Ben?

Marie: that guy in West Africa. How are the kids?

Medic: ic. They are still sick. So are you booking the flight? I know how you like shaved parts!

Marie: only if you're dumping me!

Medic: sorry for the distractions, I'm on the phone and the kids are ripping the house apart.

Marie: it's okay. At your place?

Medic: Nope their place

Marie: Is that the place you hope to get back?

Medic: What do you mean?

Marie: is it the house you had together

Medic: yeah, we have an extra bedroom here that is where I slept last night. I have been thinking about moving back in but I just don't want her to think that it means anything. It would be really nice to be close to the kids you know.. or maybe you don't?

Marie: If you did I wouldn't see you anymore

Medic: She really has big problems with working long hours and getting them to daycare and stuff...DON'T SAY THAT! I do really like you a lot and want to see you more. I feel really shitty about not seeing you very often.

Marie: If the kids are such problems for her maybe you should have them all the time. Does your family hope that the two of you will work things out and get back together?

Medic: LOL, I could never handle them and working 3 jobs and with what I do, and yes my parents hope we get back. I think she tells my daughter to bug me about coming back and that really hurts.

Marie: So being back under the same roof would help this how????

Medic: I could see them everyday, bring them to and from daycare and not have to have them alone on weekends and lots of stuff, things are not going good living with my friend, he has 2 kids of his own and his wife doesn't like me much

Marie: you are the one that said you wanted to be more than just a plaything, now you are going to hurt me

Medic: I don't want to hurt you. Maybe we can do something tonight and talk

Marie: maybe

Medic: Maybe?!

Marie: fyi...I'm sitting here in tears already

Medic: Lets at least talk about it, you really don't know how much I like you do you. I think that you are the nicest, sexiest person I have ever met, honestly...are you there?

Marie: I'm not trying to be a bitch about anything...it just hurts because out of all the guys I've met in the last two years, something seems really different about you, just some unspoken bond kind a thing

Medic: I feel it too

Marie: so????

Medic: I will leave the kids with my ex tomorrow instead of taking care of them and we can spend the whole night together, okay?

Marie: all night?

Medic: yup, the evening we can watch movies or go out for dinner, and I can stay the night

Marie: I would love that, makes me crazy when you can't ever stay long

Medic: I don't like leaving either

Marie: is it tomorrow yet?!

Medic: I wish it was. I better go take care of the kids. I will see you tomorrow.. around...6?

Marie: sounds great! <kisssssssesss>

Medic: bye

The next day came and I ran around picking up my house and making sure all the candles in the bedroom were ready for a romantic evening. Six o'clock came and went and than I finally got a phone call. Something about problems with the ex and the kids and he would get to my house as soon as possible. I started feeling like I was about the dumbest woman on the planet...believing I'd finally found a good man, with a good job, and the bonus of two young kids that really seemed to like me. The phone rang again. It was already after 10pm. But he was on his way.

I was disappointed that once again we wouldn't be going out in public anywhere and my friends still wouldn't get to meet the mystery man that I couldn't quit talking about, but we would have an entire night together and he didn't have to work until noon so we could hang out in bed most of the morning and I could bring him breakfast and spoil him. He came to my door seeming a little frazzled but wrapped his arms around me and kissed me and that was all that mattered. We fit together so perfect. It was amazing having him sleeping next to me and I looked forward to the time when it would be every night.

He woke up and caught me staring at him. I snuggled into him and kissed his chest. He asked what time it was and I told him it was just seven and he should go back to sleep. Instead he got real nervous and starting telling me that he had forgotten all about a meeting at the hospital at eight and he had to run. I pouted while I watched him get dressed. He left anyway.

My gut started flip-flopping. He hadn't shown up for the entire evening like he'd promised, and than...he had to leave earlier than he'd said...and...he wasn't wearing what I would have considered "date" clothes. His clothes had been mostly white. White...like what nurses would wear while on duty. OMG...I had just been his 11-7 shift! I knew something was seriously wrong. Someone had thought he went to work last night...or, maybe I'm just a scorned woman that has no trust left in her.

From: Marie, To: Medic
Subject: us, Date: November 30
It meant soooooooo much to me that you spent the night last night, but I am upset you didn't get here until late...you'd said we'd have the whole morning together and...again you bolted on me. Why didn't you know about the meeting at work when you went to sleep? Why don't you want to meet any of my friends or be seen out in public with me? I know with the kids and work and everything you are very busy and I've tried so hard to be patient but it now feels like something isn't right...like...you're lying to me. R u?

I've known from the start it was dangerous to get involved with someone that's divorce wasn't final but you swore to me that you'd been apart for over a year and it was just the paperwork that is taking so long. What's the real deal? Are you/have you moved back into the house? I can't take much more of this. I care about you too much already.

(Chat 11/30)
Medic: hi sweetie
Marie: wait till you read what I sent you, than talk to me
Medic: we are super busy here tonight. I am sorry that I make you feel that way. I have not lied to you. I just have a hard time talking about things.
Marie: I've noticed
Medic: and you make me feel uneasy
Marie: why?
Medic: I just can't talk about how I feel!! Sorry, it's a personal matter
Marie: you're fucking me...isn't that personal!?!
Medic: the kids are really the only reason I struggle making choices
Marie: I don't ever expect to come before them
Medic: I am tired of making them suffer for my problems
Marie: you really think somehow they are suffering?
Medic: yes, I do
Marie: and moving back is going to make it all better?
Medic: I don't know
Marie: from my perspective...if I had split with my now ex when Amber was small, she may still have a relationship with her dad, but since she grew up watching our messed up relationship and she watched him hurt me...she hates him now.
Medic: I love you Marie. I don't want to hurt you, I just don't know what I am going to do.
Marie: just please be honest with me, that's all I can ask
Medic: I have not been open but I have been honest
Marie: I know
Medic: well it's not a good time for me to talk I have to get back to work
Marie: anytime it gets slow tonight call and talk to me, it would make me feel much better

Medic: I don't feel good about calling really late

Marie: it would make me feel better because I keep thinking the worst and can't sleep anyway

Medic: I don't think you slept ten minutes last night

Marie: how would you know...you were snoring <wink> but I loved having you next to me

Medic: sorry 4that, I didn't know that I do. I don't have anyone to monitor it you know

Marie: uh huh...it didn't bother me, I think I could get used to it <wink>

Medic: it's the bed!

Marie: buy me a new one than

Medic: maybe I will, but than I get to sleep on it every night too <kiss>

Marie: yummmmm...but you won't be doing that much sleeping!

Medic: gotta go. Bye

From: Marie, To: Medic
Subject: What's real.... Date: Sat, 01 Dec 2001 06:00:46
okay...you swear up and down that we will go out this weekend...now you bail on me yet again. this morning you didn't have other plans for tomorrow night and now you do??? you never answer your cell phone anymore.. and when you call half the time its from a dif number. are you living with your wife all the time now??? I try so hard to trust and not get on your ass about anything but now I feel I am just being shit on. I've had WAAAAAAAAYYY more than my fair share of shit already and I don't feel the need to go through anymore of it. If you have to work you have to work.. of course I cant be upset about that...just don't lie to me...if I catch you in a lie I will never trust you.. and if I don't trust you.. there's no damn point in seeing you. Last night I wanted a lil explanation about your supposed break up.. you wouldn't answer some things. so I suppose that means you were a lyin cheatin bastard to your wife..????? the kind of man I hate and swear to never be near? I suppose I'm just not supposed to ask.. and just leave it all alone? well I can't do that.. it eats at me and I worry and worry and worry.. worst part is that I am drawn to you and want to care about you so bad.. the walls I've put up to protect myself seem to crumble when you are around...your touch feels so right...but.... am I wrong?

I couldn't get over the feeling that Ron was lying to me. I hoped it wasn't true but decided to start asking around to find someone that knew him and could tell me that yes he wasn't living with his wife. The thing about small town life is that anyone that doesn't know everyone does at least know someone that does…and it was time I utilized that resource. Over a couple drinks I started asking an acquaintance that works in a hospital if she knew of my Ron. She had no idea so I described him, his situation, his two kids, and why I needed to know if he was real. Now I just needed to give her some time to get back to me and have my suspicions either eased or acknowledged.

From: Medic, To: Marie
Date: Tue, 4 Dec 2001 00:20:45—0800 (PST)
Hi Marie, Sorry I have not called you in a long time. I can't even tell you how many times I picked up the phone can started calling you. I just stop before it rings and I don't know why. I have been really, really sad the past few days. I miss you terrible. You are such a beautiful fun person. It just really bothers me that you don't believe anything that I say. I am not trying to deceive you! I am just confused. I know that you want to go out with me and see me more and do all this stuff. It's just hard for me to handle everything right now. I am working 2 regular jobs and a part-time job and I see my kids as much as I can brb ok, I forgot what I had said :(My point being, I am working 3 jobs and have my kids a lot. Making little time for my social life. I don't think that is fair to you. and I don't expect you to just sit around and not go out with other ppl. Although the idea really hurts me. I wonder if meeting you was a good thing or not? (I think that you have ruined me!) I will never meet anyone that can hold a candle to you. You are just too hot to handle! I have still not made up my mind about moving back into the extra bedroom at the kids house either. You know that you can always call me, and I will be there for you, no matter what we decide to do I would really still like to be good friends with you! That matters more to me now then anything. So can I take you out to lunch on Wednesday if you're still talking to me? I would really like to see you. I need a hug! I did not get a chance to re-read the last note to you before I sent it. hope it made sense? hope this one makes sense? I am a little sleep deprived lol bye ;)

From: Marie, To: Medic

Subject: I need you, Date: Tue, 04 Dec, 15:17:06
<smoooooooooch>

ok.. I hoped all night that the phone would ring and it would be
you...but I woke up and first thing was to check here for a note
(same thing I've done everyday since we've been "together") and I
was so glad to see that there was something
from you :) :) :) :) :)
don't EVER just disappear on me again.. I cant stand it!!!!!!!!!!.. I've
been so upset and sad and my friends haven't known what to do
with me. They don't like to see me get like that and they know the
only reason I did was because I care about you sooooooo much. Of
course I did get advice on what to do about the whole situation..
most common one was to get away from you until you pulled your
head out of your ass and realized how great I am ;) (I wont tell you
the others since that's my favorite.. ;)) at the same time they all
know that if I want to be with you I cant just leave it alone and
ignore you...I don't like playing that game.
I realize that you are very busy and have a lot on your plate already
but why don't you consider that you may have met me for a reason
and that I could quite possibly help you through it all. I don't need
a lot of your time face to face (but id like it) what I really need is
just to know that you care and that you are thinking of me as
much as I'm thinking about you.
I hope to hear from you and hold you again ASAP
...thinking of you constantly, Marie

I was daydreaming at work when I got the report from my spy. She apologized for having it take a few days and than explained why, "I finally found him, but the reason I had some trouble is because he has been lying to you about his name, it's Ron McKinny not Ron McMillon, he isn't a nurse he is an aid, and everyone he works with says that yes he is still very married and does have two small children. I'm sorry."

My guts churned and I had that all to familiar ache. I let yet another lying cheating son-of-a-bitch do his little dance all over my heart. I completed a white pages search online using his real name and just like that I had Ron & Diane McKinny's home address...just twenty-two short miles from my house in a city ten miles from the city he'd professed living in with his friend. I also had their home phone number, which I called about 30 seconds after finding it. Ron's voice was on their answering machine letting me know that they couldn't take my call. I was livid. I didn't leave a message.

I tried to find my ground enough to brace for the oncoming battle. I dialed Ron's cell.

"Hi, hun," he answered.

"Hi...how are you today?" I pretended to care when I was wishing he'd tell me some nutcase at work had ripped his cock off of his body in some horrible accident.

"I'm fine and you?"

"Oh, I'm just losing my mind I guess...seems I forget things. Things like...your name for instance. What is your last name?"

"It's McMillon."

"Hmm, I had remembered correctly. Damnedest thing though there is a guy named Ron McKinny that has your voice on his answering machine."

<Loooooooooooooooooooooooooong pause>

"Well...I...ummm...I guess my ex hasn't changed her answering machine message since I left."

"Yeah, right...because us divorcee's LOVE having reminders like our ex's voice in our homes after he has left us." I snapped back at him not believing that he still was attempting a cover up!

"I don't think she knows how to change it so that must be why."

"So why have you been saying your name is McMillon and not McKinny??"

"It was McKinny but my lawyer had me change it to McMillon for business purposes, I gotta run for a minute, call you right back."

"Okay, bye." I hung up the phone almost smiling at how that lying piece of shit had to of been scrambling to figure out what I knew and what I'd done about it. I didn't think I'd hear from him again and than my phone rang...with the caller ID showing he was calling from what I had just learned was his house phone.

"Hi, umm...it's me," said Ron the fuckhead.

"Well hellooooo...still have a key to your wife's house I see."

"What? Oh, umm yes, it in case of emergencies."

"Yes, of course, and you have one now don't you. You had to get to that answering machine to see if I'd left your wife any friendly little messages."

"I don't want her to get upset."

"You don't seem to give a shit if I'm upset."

"Yes I do. I..."

"You…have until 9pm this evening to come clean with your wife over the bullshit you've been pulling on me or I will call and fill her in on all the gory details."

"I will call you later."

"You better," and with that I ended our conversation. I don't think I'd relaxed enough to breath during our little talk. I just tried so hard to be strong and not have some weepy meltdown that he could on some level enjoy.

I drove home from work crying and singing my heart out…"Love stinks…yeah, yeah."

Nine o'clock came and went without a word from my sweet lover boy. I called his home number. I got a recording, "The number you are trying to reach has been disconnected and is no longer in service." OMG!!! What an ASSHOLE! In less than four hours time he has changed his home phone number! I called his cell phone and big surprise he didn't answer it. I left him a message with some colorful adjectives.

It was only about 9:30pm so I decided that I would not let him win this battle of keeping me from contacting his wife tonight. I started driving. In less than half an hour I was parked in front of a new house on the edge of town. The lights were all off inside the house and the lights in front of the garage had colored bulbs in them for Christmas. A little wooden plaque had ivy wrapped around it with the message, Santa Stop Here. How fucking cute.

I sat in my truck just staring at it. How had he gotten her to agree to change their home phone number? What had he done with his family for the night? Were they hiding inside pretending not to be home until the crazy lady in the big blue dodge disappeared? Had he made up some excuse and whisked his little wifey off to a hotel for the night? Was it only a matter of minutes before the police came and hauled my psychotic stalking ass off to jail? I looked up and down the block and noticed that none of the neighbors were out and about either. It started feeling like some Twilight Zone episode where the main character wakes up to find they're the only person left. Deciding that I couldn't get off that easy I penned a note and left on the front door: *Would you like to know why your husband changed your home phone number today?? I'd love to tell you, Call my Cell—555-6569, Marie.*

I took my sorry ass back home, aware that the chances of Diane seeing my note were slim to none, but still happy that I left it. If nothing else it may keep Ron on his toes knowing that I knew where his house was.

From: Marie, To: Medic
Subject: Re, Date: Wed 12/05 11:27 PM
I keep going through all the things we've talked about...rereading the convos from online (yes I keep them)...looking for truth...answers...sincerity...honesty...wondering how in the hell I got taken advantage of yet again. when I'd question things some friends would say.. open your heart...let him in take a chance.. forget all the horrible crap you've been through and give him a chance. so I did. you win.. you got me...I fell for it congratulations. ggeeezzz.. I just read it all again.. it sounded honest.. you liked me.. I didn't know how much you liked me.. you loved me.. you wanted me to change my profile.. you didn't like the thought of me even chatting other men...hmmmm.. all crap??? I added everything you wrote me last night onto this message.. maybe you want to reread it too and be extra proud of yourself or keep it to send to one of your other women. I'd still like to hear from you...give you a chance to...I don't know...make me feel better...kiss my ass...or dig your grave deeper.. I'm not sure...I just want to hear something. Write me back...call me...if I don't hear from you I think you have a good idea what I'll do. bye4now...sad over you, Marie

The next afternoon I went to a girl friends house and told her what was going on in my fucked up poor excuse for a life. She felt bad for me, or at least she acted like she did. I felt I needed to even the score with Ron...I wanted to do something...something to make him hurt too. I admitted to Laura that I had in fact drove to Ron (and his wife's) house the night before and left a note on her pretty little perfectly decorated house. She looked at me like I'd gone off the deep end. Maybe I had.

I picked up my cell phone and called information. Laura's eyes got big when I asked for the numbers of two large local companies. I wrote them down and she asked, "What do you think you're going to do?"

"I'm going to call and ask to speak to Diane McKinny," I resounded.

"And what are you going to tell her?"

"I'm going to offer to tell her the truth if she wants to hear it."

"Why do you want to hurt her?"

"It isn't about hurting her, which I'm sure it will, but what it is about is informing her and letting her make her own decision. I wish someone had called and told me what Dickhead had been up to. It may have saved me months...even years of hell."

My hands shook as I punched in the phone number. The receptionist answered and I asked for Diane McKinny. No luck, she didn't have any employees with that name. I apologized and dialed the second number. This time I was instantly patched through to her office. She answered her phone and I hesitated.

I took a deep breath, "Excuse me but are you the Diane McKinny that lives in Woodpark, your husbands name is Ron?"

"Yes, I do, why" she asked.

"I met your husband online almost two months ago. He said you were getting a divorce and that he wasn't living with you anymore…" it came tumbling out of my mouth and just like that I felt empty.

"We are NOT getting a divorce, we are very much still married and of course he lives with me. You leave him alone and stay away from my family!"

"Wait, I am not the one that started this, he was chasing me and making me promises, if I had known he was married I would have never been with him…and…yes, I have BEEN with him. He's even told me that he loves me…he's had your children to my house! He used YOUR children as pawns to get in deeper with me!"

"You leave my family alone."

"I have no intention of ever seeing him again. I just found all this information out and since I was cheated on when I was married I thought you deserved to know what your husband has been up to, you can ask any questions you want," I tried to hold back the tears, I wanted her to understand.

"I don't know who you are or why you are bothering my family. We are married and we are staying that way, I don't want to hear anything else you have to say."

"Than the only other thing I have to say is, good luck, because you're going to need it, but if you change your mind and need proof call my number that I left on your door last night." I hung up my phone and sat on the couch dazed and confused. I had given Ron an almost twenty-four hour heads up that he had been busted. I had no idea what he had told his wife about me. I'm sure by now his story was that I was just some crazy woman he'd treated at the hospital that had…gained access to his personal records…or something.

"You okay?" Laura asked.

I had almost forgotten where I was and that I wasn't alone, without looking up I mumbled, "I will be." I stared at the phone in my hand, I could hear the cold harsh words of the wife of the man I thought was going to be my husband. *We're still married and we're going to stay that way.*

"What did she say?"

"She said that I should stop bothering her family."

"I'm sorry, but what did you think she was going to say to you?"

"I don't know, I guess I thought she would want to know details so she would know the truth."

"Maybe she already knows the truth. Maybe this is something he has done to her before."

That made sense to me. She didn't want the gory details because she was going to stay married. She wanted to keep her family together. She had her good job, her gorgeous new house, her adorable little son and her beautiful daughter…and her handsome, cheating piece-of-shit husband. I guess as long as his wandering ways didn't come back to her face to face it was something she tolerated, hell maybe she did the same thing to him. It could even be some sick game they played. I just didn't understand why I had to be caught up and hurt in it.

I went back home and gathered up all my Ron conversations and emails. I cried as I reread how interested in me he had claimed to be. I packed everything into an envelope and decided to have it sent to his wife at her office. I even printed another copy of Matt and Kelly riding my horse Sandy while Ron stood holding the lead rope beaming from ear to ear. I wondered how she was feeling at that moment, I wondered how she'd feel when she saw the photos I took of her children being happy at my farm. Was she as hurt and betrayed as I'd been when I found out Dickhead was fucking Secreho or was she just frustrated Ron hadn't been smart enough to keep his ho from irritating her at work. I put the envelope filled with yet another failed relationship into my file cabinet. I wouldn't send it to her unless she tracked me down and wanted it for personal or divorce court reasons.

The Christmas presents I'd bought for Mark and Kelly taunted me from the corner of my living room. As I sat in my old recliner weighed down with guilt and a patchwork quilt, I thought of how I wouldn't get to see them open the games I'd picked out for them. How I would never get to hear them refer to me as mom. I hoped Kelly would think of me as dad's friend that let her ride a horse…I hoped she'd ask to come see me again over and over just so he'd remember what he lost.

Sexual impotence is not hereditary, but impotence in the male either so complete that he cannot perform the act or consisting only in premature ejaculations should constitute a bar to marriage. This impotence may not interfere with impregnation; the wife may have children and the children will not be in any way defective, but the wife herself, unless she is completely frigid, will suffer the tortures of hell, and may quickly become a sexual neurasthenic, a nervous wreck, or she may even develop a psychosis.

Woman: Her Sex and Love Life

Squeal & Squirt

Why does a bad kisser not realize they are a bad kisser? I really don't get it. I mean if I were to kiss someone and their hands were instantly placed on my chest to keep me from getting closer...well ok, in my case the hands are usually placed on my chest as soon as they have a chance...but back to the kissing thing—if you're kissing someone and they push you away from them STOP whatever you were doing because obviously the recipient of your undesired affections has issues with your methods. Quite possibly I have turned into Picky Kisser Bitch who is rarely satisfied but come on guys, its not that difficult!

*   *   *   *   *

The online dating service had given me a lot of leads on finding Mr. Right and after many conversations I thought I had found a real treasure. In D.C. there lived a forty-year-old single attorney that was ready to settle down. He was handsome, athletic, tall and without baggage! A real find! We chatted and than lost touch a few different times over a year and than I heard from him again in the spring. It all felt fun and safe and I considered him a friend but left the possibility of more wide open.

April 3.

SnSGuy: Hi Marie! I love the new pic that's up with you and your "stud" he is a gorgeous horse!

Marie: Thanks Rob! How have you been? And yes trading my husband for that horse was the best deal I ever made!! YEEHAWWW!

SnSGuy: lol...you have a great sense of humor—I'm sure the stud will eventually pay out better than the ex! LOL

Marie: He's already been cheaper!!! He's an easy keeper...that other jerk cost me way more than he was worth! Geeezzzzz, some foreign guy just complimented me on my nice cow, umm...I'm not going to bother to reply to him.

SnSGuy: your cow??? What, did he miss the other 2 photos??? He must really be foreign if he doesn't recognize a horse from a cow! LOL well, sounds like you got the better of that trade! Hehehe

Marie: do you get hit on here by foreign women that want to come to the USA? I've blocked most other countries because I was getting marriage proposals from Ali, Mohammad, and those India guys that all look the same (who seem to worship not only cows but large redheads)...LOL, I've left Europe and Australia, I'd like an all expense paid trip there yet...hehehe.

SnSGuy: no, I have excluded all continents except North America, did not want to deal with that and besides, I am a guy—I have to pay so those women can have a free trip to the US! Not this boy! LOL

Marie: HAHAHA, good point! I've had offers to travel but the best offers come from the creeeeeepiest men so...nope...not going there...yet. Have you dated anyone that has lived close to you through here? I've done that a couple times, one was just playing not sure what the other was doing but it got weird and I haven't seen him again.

SnSGuy: I have gone out with a few women that live close to me but have been unsuccessful in the dating area—most of them are here for just fun! They are just playing and I don't like games. I have had some weird ones lately too from here and from other states.

Marie: oh so you flying them in or are you going to them? I think the majority of people online are mental...LOL...when I find someone intelligent and fun I'm always surprised. BTW, I just checked out your new pic and you are still so handsome!!! Woohoooooooooo

SnSGuy: thank you! There are a lot of mental people online, that is true! No, I don't fly them in anymore, I go there and get a hotel and an open-ended ticket! The last time I offered to fly one from FL to VA she went ballistic on me and threw away the ticket.

May 3
SnSGuy: Hi! How r u today?
Marie: Terrible…sad…crying…I just got in from morning chores and finding a dead horse.
SnSGuy: oh no I am so sorry, Marie…was this the one that just gave birth? How did it happen? I wish I could do or say something to cheer you up ☺
Marie: she was my favorite baby born last year, Trouble, and the name fit. She was turned out with a halter on and it caught the corral panel and she pulled and twisted until the panel tightened her halter enough to suffocate her ☹ now I am blaming myself for being a bad mommy.
SnSGuy: you can't blame yourself, and you are definitely not a bad mommy to your horses from what I perceive. You can't be everywhere at once, monitoring and protecting them 24/7. sometimes bad things happen and it is nobody's fault., but things happen for a reason and we mourn and then we accept the reality that we cannot change the situation and move on
Marie: I know, guess I just need to be sad for awhile, I've gotten pretty used to people/animals I care about dying, its sad that I have basically adapted to it. What about you? Any happy news? Is the woman from Indiana working out?
SnSGuy: that is a very depressing attitude to take, Marie. You need to go out and have some fun! ☺ maybe the guy from NY will cheer you up? Let's see…happy news…well I got the part I needed for my computer…and the girl from Indiana is flying in tonight to visit for the weekend, it will be our first real time alone together for an extended amount of time, so we shall see what happens???
Marie: you do have happy news ☺ I wish you luck. I know I'm just a mess, I need to take care of a bunch of things and get back on track. I don't know about my NY guy, I was really planning on breaking it off with him but maybe he is good for me.
SnSGuy: why do you say that? If you were planning on breaking it off with him, why do you think he may be good for you? You are not just settling for something (anything?) are you? You are an incredible person and you deserve what your heart desires. ☺
Marie: I don't plan on "settling" it's just that I've been hurt so much that I don't trust my heart. This man has never done anything to give me a bad feeling about him, he always makes me feel great but when we were face to face I didn't feel that magic that I expect/want to feel

when I'm with the one I think I'm seeking...but on the other hand...maybe it is just foolish of me to expect to find that.

SnSGuy: well, I guess I am rather foolish too because that is what I want to see and feel as well and maybe it doesn't happen the very first time, but after a couple of times I think you know if you will ever feel it with that person and my feeling is, if you don't then you can be friends at least and continue searching for the one ☺ I am going to have lunch now but I will come back later this afternoon if you are around. I won't log off though, okay?

Marie: okay, thank you for your ear Rob. <kiss> I wish you luck and "the one"

May 8

Marie: Hey stud!! How was your wild weekend with Miss Indiana?? Did you get some...hehehe

SnSGuy: It was good and yes...I did get some but I'm not sure how into me she was.

Marie: why do you say that? What did she say? What happened?

SnSGuy: we had some incredible sessions—and she would tell me how wonderful I made her feel and how much she enjoyed it with me...

Marie: hmm, I usually will just avoid the subject when it's been bad so she must have liked it.

SnSGuy: my perception is that most women will avoid the subject or treat it like a chore if it is not any good...but hey I am SmartnSexyGuy...;)

Marie: lol...damn and I had shortnnosparks4me guy here...waaahhh-hhhhhh

SnSGuy: I am sure that was not his profile name but maybe you could suggest it to him and cite to the Truth in Advertising Laws? LOL but let's not be too harsh—you mean that he was short in height compared to you?

Marie: yes he is 5'5 and I was trying sooooo hard not to judge him for it. We joke constantly about me being his huge bitch...lol...and I make "small" comments about him all the time! It's fun, but...I wish we had just stayed friends and not tried to have it be more ☹ there just aren't sparks there for me and dammmmittt I want SPARKS!!!!

SnSGuy: that is why I try not to cross that threshold if I do not have the physical attraction at least. It almost sounds like you went there because you felt like you should because he came out there or because you wanted to see if maybe you could "force" something to happen that would create the "sparks"!

Marie: yeah…I did try to force it some. That's part of why I was attempting to save you from making the same mistake I did. I loved his smile, his eyes, and the way he made me feel when we chatted and talked, but…guess he still wasn't the one, and yes…I tried to force it a little because I felt guilty about usually not even dating anyone shorter than I am, and who says my soul mate is taller than me…just because I hope he is…if you know what I mean…ps.. your soul mate could be a huge redheaded farm girl…lol. You just never know.

SnSGuy: and I would not have any problems with that…does she have any new photos?? ;) okay, I'm leaving work now and heading home, catch you later <kiss>

*   *   *   *   *

Our conversations continued and we discussed our relationships. His Indiana woman didn't work out and I realized I couldn't make my NY friend the love of my life. I wanted to run away from my problems and Rob invited me to hang out with him a few days. Tickets were cheap and we both had the holiday weekend open so I made plans to fly to D.C. and vacation at Robs place.

I was excited about my weekend in D.C. and the timing of having it be Memorial Day made it that much better. My plane was delayed which made my scheduled late night arrival an early morning arrival. While I fussed with my makeup I worried that Rob would be upset after waiting so long, not a very good way to start my fun filled vacation. I know this meeting has been set up as two friends hanging out and just having fun but of course I always go into meeting a new man with at least a faint hope that he could be The One!

Rob met me with a smile and a light hug and I apologized for my plane being late. I searched his face to see if he was upset, tired or not interested in me and I couldn't decide one way or the other. On the shuttle to baggage claim he held my hand and moved in to kiss me. I drew back a bit and he kept coming. His soft lips pressed onto mine, and the voice in my head thought, hmm I guess he isn't repulsed by me. It was just an instant later when I remembered there were many other people in the shuttle and some of them must have been watching us. I was going to settle back into the stiff vinyl bench seat when I was violated by darting lizard-like tongue. I pushed away and he pulled me closer. I tried to adjust a bit to this strange in and out icky tongue darting maneuver. I was grossed out, but…he was handsome, a lawyer, single and I was away for the weekend so I would make the best of it. We picked up my baggage and headed for his car. It was almost 2am and the parking lot was quiet. He lifted my bag to his trunk and I noticed a couple men walking through the lot. Rob grabbed me again and began groping my ass and assaulting me with his darting lizard tongue. Every time the tongue flicked into my face I pushed him back but in D.C. or lawyer-land that seems to be the signal to pull the woman closer and repeat the tongue offensive. A couple minutes passed and I noticed the other men were gone. The tongue was retracted and he opened the car door for me. I slid in and made sure my skirt fell so when he got in he couldn't help but notice the legs he had admired in the photos I had sent him. I struggled to get a conversation going on the way to his apartment and still wasn't sure he was even glad I was there.

His apartment was tiny. True I am spoiled by wide-open spaces and privacy but I kept thinking a single attorney that was forty should have had a nicer place. I excused myself to the bathroom to freshen up and put on a silky long gown that I thought was tasteful yet sexy. That way we could sit on the couch and visit for a while and keep it just friends yet…like the plan.

I came out of the bathroom to find most of the lights out and Rob standing in just his boxers. He had been what I thought was cold to me except for the gropeathons and here in his apartment there was no one for him to show off to so I had figured I was safe. He asked if I was ready to sleep since it was late and he was tired and he motioned to his bed. I was tired and decided that since it was the only bedroom in the house maybe he did actually mean to sleep. I know it is possible to sleep in the same bed without having sex with a man and I could handle that. I'd leave the long gown on and it would be innocent enough.

I crawled under the covers and said goodnight. He did the same. I looked around in the dark trying to figure out what different shapes were and the little voice worked on deciphering if the man laying next to me liked me or not. I'd probably only been there a couple minutes when he rolled over and kissed me. He pulled me close and rolled me on top of him. The little voice dropped its abacus. Again the lizard tongue darted in and out of my mouth and my attempts at training him to kiss differently were failing miserably. I sat up on him, still in my gown and he in his boxers. I ran my hands along his chest and he pulled me back down to kiss me some more. The little voice had an idea. I kissed his chin and than down on his neck. He shivered and made a strange noise. I decided that the neck kissing was working for him and since it kept his nasty tongue out of my mouth I would do it again. I got a little more aggressive and bit his neck a bit with my kissing. He squealed. I had never heard a man make a noise like that before and the little voice was impressed with itself. I kissed his neck again and he squirmed a bit but was quiet. The little voice stopped in its tracks and screamed inside my head-Oh My Gawd! Did what I think just happen really happen??? Is it over? Is he done? I sat up and tried to see his face in the darkness and the little voice swore to tell all my friends about this squeal and squirt attorney guy in D.C. He grabbed my arms and rolled me off of him and back onto my side of the bed. Without saying a word he got out of bed and went to the bathroom. After running some water he returned to the bedroom in fresh boxers and casually tossed his smiley face boxer shorts into the laundry hamper just a few feet from me. He crawled back under the covers and with his back to me seemed to fall asleep instantly. I lay in the darkness 1100 miles from home staring at the barely visible yellow smiley faces taunting me from the hamper and reminiscing fondly of sex that actually involved penetration.

So much for men not making passes
At girls that wear glasses.

Our actions are under our control, to a certain extent at least, and if we do a bad or injurious act, we have committed a sin and are morally responsible. The desire for the sexual act is no more sinful than the desire for food is when one is hungry. But the performance of the act may, under certain circumstances, be as sinful as the eating of food which the hungry man obtained by robbing another fellow-being, just as poor as himself.

Woman: Her Sex and Love Life

The Married Man

I know what you're thinking…MARRIED??? Yes…I have to admit to it. The one thing I prided myself on avoiding. The line I swore I'd never cross. Yet I crossed it. I looked at it, walked up and down it, backed away from it and then eventually ignored all the caution and danger signs and leaped right over the fucking thing.

It started simply enough. A brief email at the naughty sight.

Saw your profile and you sound interesting. Perhaps we could share somethings and find out a little about each other. If you'd like to tell me…
1) What's in your car CD player
2) Favorite Vacation
3) Favorite leisure activity (non-sex)
4) What do you want/need to do today?

I looked up his profile and found him older than I normally consider, forty-five, but intelligent, educated and I felt some sincerity in his words. Looking back I notice he hit me with some of my "tag" words: *good conversation, inner beauty, passionate, intensity, humor, intimate, I'll listen, friendship, excitement and prefer someone who has natural beauty.* Yup, tag…I was it.

The letter was simple enough. I thought it to be intro spam he probably sent to every woman twenty-five to fifty and within one hundred miles. Yet I played along and decided to respond. Question one…good question really. Its safe, simple and even the most brain dead bimbo on the sight should be able to answer. Better than the fact that it's simple is the fact that it is non-sexual. He resisted the temptation to write down the question going through the tiny minds of the average male, which is—1) Would you suck on my cock and swallow my load on our first date? I know any single women that have dated a lot are nodding their heads and the ones that don't have a life are disgusted and thinking that's not true but the men are all smiling in agreement.

I'm not sure I answered truthfully because my musical tastes vary so greatly when driving. I go from AC/DC to Eminem to Disney Favorites to Dolly to the Soundtrack from Cats. Since he was older than me and I didn't want to freak him out to badly I answered—Wynonna's Greatest Hits. I answered the others truthfully...oh wait, I did not answer number three with eating half a pan of brownies with a big glass of milk while watching Blazing Saddles. Finding out quaint little quirks like that is what marriage is all about...right?

I sent him the message and didn't think about it too much. I had other letters I sent replies to and younger fish to fry. He sent a couple more notes to me, still no sexual requests just casual...*how was your weekend, you are beautiful, hope to talk to you soon.*

I like kind but not pushy. Gives the illusion of being attentive. Then I received this little gem that I didn't respond too.

It's cold but my cock is long and hard. Did you know that my favorite thing to do is lick pussy until my partner shudders with ecstasy? I've become quite an expert at pleasing. Just being honest...on this cold winters night.

It may have been around this time that I got the email with the photo attached. It showed a middle aged balding man pointing at the camera like...gotcha...or maybe its some foreign man speak that I have not yet learned. I'm not sure what the pointy finger thing was intended to represent, but as far as I'm concerned, stick out your thumb and put that big L up to your forehead buddy...no way am I going out in public with you!

I didn't hear anymore for about a week than:

A proposition...I'm headed to Orlando this weekend for a few days, I have business there next week. Are you interested in coming along for a couple of days as a traveling companion? Expenses would be covered and it is sure to be a fun filled adventure. Think about it...have you ever been truly spontaneous! Let me know and I'll book the flight.

This appealed to not only my curiosity, more importantly my desire to have some heat! Not the heat of a man…umm…nonexistent most times anyway…but sunshine!!! Dear sweet golden rays of pure love! <sigh> Ahhh, live in Minnesota for a winter and you'll know just how attractive anything over forty degrees can be. I hadn't even met the man face to face and he had just become more appealing than anyone I was considering seeing. Err, at least more appealing than anyone within a few hundred mile radius!

I hesitated a couple days before responding and telling him that I'd like to talk on the phone and get a better feel for how we would get along. When my phone rang later that night it was him. I guess since he didn't even give me his real name I can use his own self assumed name and here on call him Pete. Pete had a warm friendly voice and I fell into it like my favorite old recliner. We shared our lives and hopes and fears and pains from past relationships. A brief moment of silence only occurred when I think we both were asking ourselves why we were sharing so much so soon. It was almost like ripping open your chest and pulling out your heart. Plopping it down on the table in front of a total stranger…than realizing maybe it wasn't such a good idea to be so exposed and yet…nothing I could do about it now. Might as well discuss that oozing mess that's been staining and distorting my moral fiber.

Churning up hurtful things from my past didn't sting as much as it used to. It's much easier now to see what I have learned and how much better off I truly am. I talked some of my dating history and made sure to bring up the McMarried McBastard story. It's a pretty sure fired way to get a married man to leave you alone. Since Pete took it in stride I told myself that he must not be married. Than he confessed that actually he was still married but that his wife had been having an affair with a doctor for quite sometime and he was going to be moving on.

I know…the line was there. I saw it. Yet I wet my finger and rubbed it until it blurred into something resembling more of a hazy cloud than a line.

We talked on the phone almost every day. I didn't go on the trip with him but he called me in the evenings to discuss what he had done each day. I told myself we'd just be friends and I'd help him see how he either needed to fix his marriage or end it and move on. He listened and cared about the details of my life. It was nice.

We decided to meet and hang out for an evening and just have fun together. I suggested supper at a local strip club where they have good steaks. He couldn't believe that it wouldn't bother me to go to a strip club. I said I loved the people watching and the other tits there were never as nice as mine anyway…why should I be upset?!

I waited in a bar near the strip club. I was nervous but figured it would just be a fun night. No stress, no sex, just hanging with a new friend. I did however wear the curve clinging button all the way down the front sweater dress and boots that I'd been complimented on the last time I wore out. The voice in the back of my head kept repeating...*how could anyone go out with another mans husband, what kind of slut meets a married man, if you hang out with a married man you are just asking for trouble, going anywhere date-like with a married man is like running through a fireworks factory with two torches and being surprised when shit blows up!*

A few minutes later a tall well built man with a charismatic smile walks up to me. He apologizes for being late, tells me how gorgeous I look and pulls from his coat a single red rose. He hands me the rose and gives me a nice long hug. I have on heels yet he is still slightly taller and his long arms wrapped around me feel good. We talk about our daughters over drinks all very well and friend like.

The strip club is packed but luckily we grab a small table as two others leave. I feel the men watch me wondering what I'm doing there and I love it. Pete pulls out my chair and still has that great smile spread all across his face. Glancing around I see a half dozen women doing lap dances to mostly young college men. I watch as Pete looks quickly but returns his longing gazes to me. A strip club may seem like the oddest place for a date but I think it saves a lot of time. Obviously there are other women there for your date to check out...and he doesn't even have to imagine what they look like naked...he pretty much gets to see that right than, but...if he can look at them for a bit and still hold a conversation with you...and still look at you and keep telling you how incredibly stunning you are...he's worth spending some of your time on.

As we sip our drinks and wait for the steaks we enjoy the music and the people watching. A few feet away a pretty young brunette spanks her own ass for the unwashed older patron just inches away from something he could never really have. She smiles when she notices us watching her. Most of the dancers seem to like having other women in the audience. (Yes, they do hit on me occasionally. I really don't mind it's better than not being hit on.) Her fingers move up and fiddle with her tiny almost boyish breasts and I nudge Pete, "See I told you none of them would have tits like mine."

He looks around the bar at the other dancers and laughs in agreement, "You're right...not even close."

I lean back and breath a bit deeper. Letting the buttons pull a bit on my sweater. Heaving mounds of cleavage rise and fall slightly. I turn so I more squarely face Pete and cross my legs making sure the unbuttoned lower part of my dress falls open revealing most of my inner thighs. I sit back and the voice in my head screams...*OH MY GAWD THE TORCHES ARE LIT THE TORCHES ARE LIT!* I think...oh shut up little voice, just because the torches are lit doesn't mean any of the damn fireworks will go off.

Pete dares to put his hand on my mostly exposed thigh and then looks deeply into my eyes. I keep eye contact with him and lean in to him letting my forehead touch his. Then we tip our heads and kiss...soft wanting lips. Slow kisses as I feel his hand come up and cradle my cheek. I try to breath as my head falls lightly onto his shoulder. I melt and he takes my hand. Looking down I notice his freckled arm and strawberry blonde hairs. His hands are big but not rough. It feels like it's just us on the planet even though we are surrounded by others.

After the most incredible steaks and light hearted conversation. Usually dealing with one of the girls cottage cheese legs or asking each other what's not quite right with the face on the one over there? Sorry but you have to make sure both of you realize no one is perfect...hahaha...we decide to leave the strip club to bar hop.

We take his nice expensive vehicle and I wonder how he could possibly ever explain the long red hairs that will inevitably be left behind somewhere. The little voice wants to pull some extra ones out and shove them places where they wouldn't be missed but I don't let it. I hold onto his arm as we walk to and from different bars. It seems so proper and nice. Maybe it's just the difference between dating boys and men...I'm not sure.

A battle goes on in my head. I'm upset with myself for liking him so much. Yet I'm wondering if I'm letting myself like him so much because it's so impossible. You know me and impossible situations, the damn things are like drugs to me. Worst it could be the more I'm going to want it. I admit to myself that I would have sex with him.

His sensor must have picked up on this because just like that he asks if we should try to find a hotel room somewhere. I just smile and nod and my little voice kicks me. I wait in the car while he goes to check in. I think about going through the glove box and finding personal items and I realize I don't want to find personal items. Now he's just a single man that I want more of...not someone's dad or worse...someone's husband.

Fate tries to help me out by not having an available hotel room anywhere in the city. The devil lures us to a dark parking lot where we decide making out like high-school kids would be fun. He flattens out the back seats and throws a blanket across them. I crawl over and lay there waiting for him. The little voice is pissed.

I love that little kid at Xmas look a man gets when he knows he's going to get some. I'm such a pleaser it's like knowing you have a present they've always wanted and you're just happy you can give it to them. His baseball cap falls off. The streetlight flickers off the top of his male pattern baldness. We kiss some more and I tell myself I can adjust to the hairline. The little voice giggles. We kiss some more and off come my boots and the nylons, than the dress and my pretty red bra. He tells me how beautiful I am and I'm happy he's happy. He takes off his shirt and the damn streetlights dance across the slightly sagging older man boobies. I play with my nipples and think everything is going to be okay because he really likes me.

We make out some more and it's fun that it's wrong. Wrong to be in a public parking lot naked and making out. A cheating country song plays on the radio. The little voice turns up the volume in my head and I feel guilty again. He's on top of me and I wait for more he grabs a rubber and I wait anxiously. He kisses me again and I feel him reach down to guide himself into me. I wait. I feel him bump against me and I wait. I start to think...oh my fucking gawd this cannot be happening to me again...and I wait.

Just like that come those words that I just LOVE to hear.. gggrrrrr.. NOT.. "ummm.. damn...I ummm.. can't belive this...this never happens to me," he sorrowfully said.

Oh yeah!! Mr Limpy is back in town. What would a hot date be without a flaccid penis! I have the worst damn luck on the planet. We frustratingly try again and again but they were feeble attempts. He was sweating like crazy as I kissed the top of his head and told him it was okay I didn't really want to have sex anyway. ***Special note to all men that have no wood. Bury your damn face between her thighs and add some fingers because just cause YOU have issues you have no right to ruin her night!

He asks me to help him try to get going again. I've never understood why at this moment in time that should be my responsibility but I reach down and diddle with droopy. It succeeds only in adding to my frustration and eventually we both give up.

As we lie there getting cold because obviously all the heat we had built up between us was now gone he looks at me and says, "I lied before, this has happened to me once before, it was the first time I was with my wife."

I'm hurt that he mentions his wife. Than that part of my brain injured by too many horse falls thinks...*wow with his wife and me...his next wife...It's kind of a compliment of some sort.* We search the darkness for our clothing and get dressed. I put my nylons in my coat pocket because straightening them back out in the dark would be futile. The ride back to the parking ramp is quiet. I feel good that I never actually had sex with him and happy that I have rigid toys waiting at home.

There is an open parking spot next to my truck and we pull in. I tell him goodbye and he says he will walk me over to my truck. I'm glad because just dumping someone off seems so cold. I put my arms up over his shoulders and kiss him. Everything is wonderful again and he feels so good. The kisses deepen and the passion is once again ignited. Fireworks must be going off because I can even feel a rocket in his pocket. I push my pelvis into his and think oh my gawd it does work!

I hug him tighter, grinding myself into him and whisper, "I left off my nylons and I'm not wearing any panties."

He grabs my hand and leads me back to the passengers side of the truck. He opens the door and sets me up on the seat. We kiss wildly while he unbuttons his pants. My boots go up over his shoulders and we fuck like animals in the incredibly well lit parking ramp. It is so naughty and hot we don't even care if anyone would happen to be watching. It doesn't last long but it's intense.

He covers his completely exposed ass and I let my dress fall back to my knees. We kiss again and I'm crawling up onto him. He apologizes for just getting me turned on and having to go. I am just thrilled that his cock can get hard. I wave goodbye as he drives away. I go home and get myself off about four times. I sleep.

Could this be the one way to keep me out of trouble?
Nawww….

A little thought will show clearly that Love is not merely sexual love, not merely a desire to gratify the sexual instinct. If love were merely sexual desire, then one member of the opposite sex, or at least one attractive member, would be as good as any other. And indeed in animals and in the lower races, where love as we understand it does not exist, this is the case. To a male dog any female dog is as good as another, and vice versa.

Woman: Her Sex and Love Life

Too Easy

I had met a man in chat one night that attempted to impress me by telling me he had a big cock, big arms, and he was tall. Unfortunately he was also a moron so I didn't believe anything he said. He had no picture but was willing to meet up for sex ASAP. It had been a slow week and I was bored so I did let him call me. At first he asked questions about me that weren't sexual and I thought I had misjudged him. A few minutes later and I was making excuses to end our conversation.

Not long after my run in with TB2000 my girlfriend in chat messaged me that she had some hottie on the line. It was TB2000. I was not impressed but somehow he managed to push enough of her buttons to get her to agree to meeting him for dinner. I warned her to be on her guard and she swore to stay in a public place. The evening came for their big dinner and I made her promise to call me from the bathroom and let me know what he was like. She called and not from the bathroom, but from her car where she waited, and waited, and waited for him to show up. I think she gave him about an hour and he was still a no show, no call. She was upset and I told her I'd help her get even.

This is one of the very few times I pretended to be someone I'm not. I changed my chat nickname to call_me, and messed with TB2000 for my friend.
call_me: what's up big boy?

TB2000: ☺:
call_me: mmmmm…hi…
TB2000: Hi, Ted, 40, single, St. Paul. You?
call_me: Erin, 30, looking
TB2000: Where you from?

call_me: Cities
TB2000: What do you look like?
call_me: you first
TB2000: Me.6:3,225,brown hair,eyes,muscular build,very hand-some!
call_me: very — really? how did you get your build? do you have pics?
TB2000: Construction worker off now, did Ice Castle. Never married, no kids. You?
call_me: ohhh mmm.. I like a man that uses his hands
call_me: i am seperated, 2 kids.. looking, but not for anything serious
TB2000: So, what do you look like? Me, neither.
call_me: 5'9, long light brown hair, athletic but curvy
TB2000: Sorry, no pic would you like together tonight? Will give you my number.
call_me: do you play often?
TB2000: No, birthday was a month ago, went to bed at 10:00p.m.,by myself!
call_me: no dates since?
TB2000: No, you?
call_me: yes i date often
TB2000: Would you like to get together tonight?
call_me: at your place?
TB2000: Yours, mine.
call_me: mine wont work
call_me: house or apt?
TB2000: apt.
call_me: phone #?
TB2000: 651 555-6940.When can you call?
call_me: how late can we meet?
TB2000: What's good for you?
call_me: I have to call a friend to come sit the kids
TB2000: Could you call me, we'll go from there?
call_me: of course
TB2000: When?
call_me: after I call my friend
call_me: I hope you're rested, I need some serious attention
TB2000: Sounds good.10-15 mins?
call_me: brb
TB2000: Could I get you're number?
TB2000: k

call_me: sorry can't do that because of my kids
call_me: what is your favorite thing to do sexually?
TB2000: Understand, when can you call me?
TB2000: Everything. Yummm! You?
call_me: i like to be on top
call_me: how "big" r u?
TB2000: Very.
call_me: well there can be too much of a good thing
TB2000: How do you want to do this?
call_me: first tell me how big.. i don't need to get hurt
TB2000: 9
call_me: that's big! how thick?
TB2000: Thick enough, haven't measured lately, you will enjoy.
call_me: when were you last tested?
TB2000: year ago, clean. You?
call_me: no sex since?
TB2000: No. You?
call_me: month for me, but I always use rubbers
call_me: have a problem with that?
TB2000: No, have some.
call_me: what kind?
TB2000: Couple differnt. You have some you like?
call_me: maybe I should pick some up, I just need to know your real size!!
TB2000: Told you. Well, how do you want to do this?
call_me: id like to come over in lingerie, no talking, just wild sex
TB2000: Sounds good. When?
call_me: what is your address?
call_me: its a fantasy of mine, handsome stranger.. no words.. me in a trench coat
call_me: id like to live it out
TB2000: 694 Jones, St. Paul, by bridge. Do you know how to get here?
call_me: i will map quest it
call_me: which apt?
TB2000: 35 to Park exit, take right at lights, next lights is Jones, take right, 3 blocks down, blue house on right, it's a house.
TB2000: When can you be here?
call_me: I think 11pm.. does that work for you?
TB2000: Fine, will leave porch door open, just knock.

call_me: and.. could you be in boxers? with candles lit
call_me: that would really be erotic
TB2000: k
call_me: i hope you're as excited as i am now, no strings, no questions, just hot sex right?
TB2000: Tell me a bit more what you look like? That's the plan.
call_me: i wear a 36d bra
call_me: 10 jeans
TB2000: So, 11?
call_me: yes!
call_me: you better be hard and ready!!
TB2000: oh I will
call_me: I'm SOOO WET JUST THINKING ABOUT IT
TB2000: Where something sexy! Stockings, etc.
call_me: you bet i will
TB2000: K hun, I will see you then.
call_me: bye4now
TB2000: bye ☺

I wonder how long that dumb ass waited for someone to knock on his door, LOL. Obviously he would have stuck his dick in whatever showed up. He had no pictures, no voice, no previous contact with "call_me" and yet he gave out his phone number, his home address and directions to his place within a couple minutes of chatting just because she was going to put out.

He did leave some offline messages for call_me over the next few days. Just wondering what had happened and if they could try again sometime. It's been over a year and occasionally he'll bump into my friend or I online and forget that he ever chatted us before. I let him show me his cam one day when I knew he didn't recognize me. He wasn't *very handsome* like he'd stated and you could tie a barbell to his thingy and it still wouldn't stretch to nine inches.

Love is the most complex, the most mysterious, the most unanalyzable of human emotions. It is based upon the difference in sex-upon the attraction of one sex for another. It is fostered by physical beauty, by daintiness, by a normal sexuality, by a fine character, by high aspirations, by culture and education, by common interests, by kindness and consideration, by pity, by habit and by a thousand other subtle feelings, qualities and actions, which are difficult of classification or enumeration.

A great love, greatly reciprocated, is in itself capable of rendering a human being supremely happy. Nothing else is. Other things, such as wealth, power, fame, success, great discoveries, may give supreme satisfaction, great contentment, but supreme, buoyant happiness is the gift of a great love only. Such loves are rare, and the mortals that achieve it are the envy of the gods. But a great love, unreciprocated, especially when admixed to it is the feeling of jealousy, is the most frightful of tortures; it will crush a man like nothing else will, and the victims of this emotional catastrophe are pitied by the inmates of the lowest inferno.

Woman: Her Sex and Love Life

Finally A Nice Guy

After emailing back and forth a couple times and chatting briefly I agreed to have a date with someone that apparently didn't live very far away from me. He was 34 never married and no kids (which makes me nervous because I don't know that I want to be popping out any more babies) but he was also ex military, traveled, and had a college degree so I figured we could at least discuss where he had traveled too.

It was a casual day date and I let him come to my house and pick me up. With all of the traveling for dates I've done it felt odd to let someone come to my house to pick me up. I think its part of my controlling the situation issues…lol…when I drive somewhere I know I can escape if need be. He pulled up in a cute little blue convertible and came to my door all nervous yet smiling. I thought he was more handsome than the photo I'd seen and his broad chest and strong arms made the fact that he was just a tad shorter than me seem like no big deal. He walked me to the car and opened the door for me and I immediately started to think that I liked him.

We talked on the way to town and it seemed to be pretty comfortable right away. I wanted to stop and apply for a job as long as we were in town and a stop at the porn store didn't seem to phase him a bit…hehehe. I wanted to see how the country boy would handle his date applying to work at a store filled with marital aids and gag gifts and he took it in stride very nicely. Next we went to the mall to see if we could catch a matinee we both agreed on a comedy and even though it wasn't a classic it was fun. He'd planned an evening at a comedy club but we had a couple hours to burn yet before the show so he suggested just going for a drive. Everywhere we went he opened all the doors and paid for everything a true gentleman and he was making more points every step of the way. He drove me around town pointing out a place he used to live and discussing where he'd served and when he went to college. It was all just so nice.

We drove out of town around the ski resort and to a park he knew. I was game for a walk and had never been there before. It was beautiful. He was so sweet and not pushy and I was having a great time. We hiked up a steep hill and found ourselves on an old bridge that had been redone to accommodate hikers and bikers. The view was amazing. A small river flowed far below and the hillsides where covered with trees. We stood there soaking in the scenery and talking about our friends and family. I remember the light breeze blowing through my hair and the warm sun on my face and a possible new love with his arm around me. I started wondering how many other women he'd brought to this great place but it didn't really matter I was glad for the day that it was my turn. He turned me toward him, looked into my eyes, touched my face and kissed me for the first time in the middle of that bridge and I knew it was a moment I would never forget. It wasn't the take my breath away stop my heart kind of kiss that I fantasize about but it also wasn't some icky lizard tongue or something I wanted to run from.

After that moment where ever we went we usually were holding hands and staying close to each other. We had dinner and watched the comedy show cuddled close together laughing at the same things…it was a great day. He drove me home the long way, and we spent a few minutes kissing good night and talking about when we'd see each other again. Luckily we both felt the same and we ended up seeing each other all but one day that first week.

I'm not sure what to tell you about this man. We just kind of stepped right into each others lives and were comfortable with that. I met his family and friends and he met mine. Everyone liked him a lot and they were happy I'd finally found someone special. We laughed and joked and teased each other without either of us having hard feelings. It was the kind of relationship that I'd hoped to find…hmmm…yes there has to be a but, but…we avoided any deep conversations relating to our relationship and where it could be headed. It was mutual avoidance of the big picture. That way with no expectations we could spend each day as it came with no stress or pressure. Neither of us saw anyone else or had any desire to as far as my part. There would have been no time to because we were together so much of the time. It was not my typical MO and I found myself wondering if looking to far ahead in my other relationships is what destroyed them.

We never spoke the "L" word. After a couple months I thought he was going to tell me that and I would have told him the same but after different events came and went without the big "L" I started to question if I even wanted to hear it. Is love the ability to spend extended amounts of time with the same person and not be fighting? Is love the desire to want to just be cuddled up with someone watching movies or just talking to each other for hours and hours? Is love comfortable? Is love "nice"?

A friend once told me to seek a slow steady burn of love instead of the sparks that I find myself drawn into. Is it wrong to want your breath taken away with a kiss? Maybe it is…but it's still what I seek. Maybe I am just like the moth that flings itself against the light bulb time and time again because it just can't resist. Driven by the lust for the light and not common sense. I think of how most of the time the bodies of the moths are eventually found below the lights and I worry for myself.

Almost 1am, Thursday October 28th

I've become obsessed with those sticky little mousetraps. I have them strategically placed throughout my house—behind the stove, on the pantry floor, on the pantry shelves and in the lazy-susan that houses the liquor safely out of sight. I check them several times a day. A recent outbreak of droppings has spurred this vigilant quest to rid my house of the tiny pests. In the last two days and nights I have been successful five times. For some odd reason I think I am fascinated with the way they are caught and their reaction to it. Some squeak, others are quiet—like a mouse—I guess. I find some stuck down like they'd belly-flopped into a waterless swimming pool, one by its back legs and tail like it had almost freed itself, another on its side. The cute little brown field mouse I discovered this morning was stuck belly to chin and it's whiskers twitched when I looked into its watery dark eyes. I carefully carried the trap to the garbage can and shoved it in amidst the other discards of my life.

I now sit in my library. A developing funky smell has brought yet another sticky trap along the walls edge. This morning while returning a few books to the shelves I had a revolting sensation. Looking down I found I had stepped onto a trap that was moved from the safe place I'd set it and now the trap and its furry little victim were both stuck on the bottom of my sock. I tugged carefully until the trap, the mouse and most of that sticky crap was off of me.

There is a man in my bed. He's been there before and I like him a lot. He is cute and sweet and does his best to not upset me. I like being around him. We can be close and its comfortable, he is quiet and silly. I find his things around my house, first a toothbrush and not long after a razor. A small pile of clothing just dropped at the end of my bed and a work uniform hung among my blouses. There is a Twins hat in my bathroom and a police cap in my living room. There is a pair of work boots just inside the entry door and other assorted droppings in my office, dining room and kitchen.

I snuck out of my bed so I wouldn't wake him. It seems I sleep less and less the more I should be getting used to his being there. Lying closely to him I watch as he twitches in his sleep. I stare at his whiskers. He half snores and breathes on me and the smell makes me wince. When his sweet kind eyes open and look at me I think about how happy I should be. Then I wonder…how big a sticky trap would it take?

*   *   *   *   *

I hadn't realized until after writing that previous piece how obviously over my relationship was. He left in the morning and I sat in my office rereading about the droppings. Later that evening we connected online and I decided to "talk" out all the concerns we never spoke of face to face. As tears spilled out my eyes I wrote of how much he'd come to mean to me and yet how something I felt I needed just wasn't there. His reaction was to agree. (I think that surprised and maybe disappointed me a little) He said he had the feeling that we were both holding each other back and he asked what we should do about it. I told him I felt that we should stop seeing each other. He was shocked. We chatted for an hour or so, both of us in tears, both of us sad to walk away but yet somehow knowing it was the right thing for us at that time.

Kind of strange for me to be so "adult" when ending a relationship, but I thought there may come a day when I'd be happy that bridge wasn't blown to bits.

November 17th

The roses blackened, dry and lifeless
Hang from a peg near my mirror
A symbol of love no longer fresh.
Does he know that I've kept them?
I wonder,
Why have I kept them?
Is it to remember what was,
Or what is.

To repeat, neuroses, neurasthenia, psychasthenia, and the various forms of neuropathy and psychopathy are dysgenic factors. But people suffering from these conditions often are among the world's greatest geniuses, have done some of the world's greatest work, and, if we prevented or discouraged marriage among people who are somewhat "abnormal" or "queer," we should deprive the world of some of its greatest men and women. For insanity is allied to genius, and if we were to exterminate all mentally or nervously abnormal people we should at the same time exterminate some of the men and women that have made life worth living.

Woman: Her Sex and Love Life

I'm Better Now…I Swear

June 26th, 9:30pm

Came down to write this last chapter. It's been six years since I first logged on to a chat room. Six years! OMG! In those years I have spent approximately two years of that time online. I have chatted tens of thousands of men from all over the planet. My contributions in cyber sex and naughty picture trading no doubt responsible for enough ejaculate to fill more than one fifty-five gallon drum. Gross I know but you do the math!

I've gotten to the point that I can just put someone on ignore if they are rude or disrespectful. I deleted my profile on the naughty sight. I don't have any personal ads posted. I don't have to connect to the internet several times a day just for the thrill of reading emails from men that want to meet me.

I have learned that no matter how messed up my life is, someone online will make me feel better. It may be a friend online that tells me they care about me. It may be a man telling me he thinks I'm pretty, or sexy, or better yet funny and intelligent. Or it may just be witnessing some pathetic soul spamming a chat room for a piece of ass and realizing I must have more control than that guy/gal.

My original instincts about the majority of men online just being a bunch of lying perverts, confirmed. True, I did meet some nice guys but they were few and far between. I really thought I would find the man of my life online. Some similarly confused soul in search of something…

A year ago today was the first date with one of the good men. I recently found out the he is marrying the woman he met after I broke up with him. I'm happy for him. Several of the men I had dated married the next woman after me. Okay, I'll admit that messes with my head a bit. Did the thought that there may be other women on the planet like me scare them into marrying the first sane woman after me? Naw...I believe instead that they found someone they could keep up with in bed and figured they better hold on to her. LOL.

I don't need a man, don't really care to have a man and I'm okay with that. I like sleeping sprawled out in the middle of my bed oblivious to whether I'll snore that night or not. I like not wearing makeup for days. I like grabbing something quick to eat that isn't good for me, and not having someone give me that you-should-know-better look. I can come online and chat occasionally without it being an addiction. I can give up the flirting and the thrill of being hit on at any time of day. I can go out locally and not wish I was back home online with my friends. I can live with not having a string of men telling me they'd like to meet me. I don't have to date. I have toys and I've learned how to use them. I...I...oh, I see a guy in the personals that looks like Owen Wilson and says he likes voluptuous women...and he only lives thirty miles from me...I...I...I need to post a new personal ad.

About the Author

Layne Underwood grew up a repressed farm girl in a very religious family. She believed in happily-ever-after. Marriage offered betrayal—disillusioned, she turned to her own dreams and the Internet. It's no wonder that when she finally stood on her own feet, her adventures were worth living and writing about.

978-0-595-37778-7
0-595-37778-5

www.ingramcontent.com/pod-product-compliance
Lightning Source LLC
Chambersburg PA
CBHW051234050326
40689CB00007B/917